OBAMA'S RING: THE SEAT OF SATAN

By

Will Clark

OBAMA'S RING: THE SEAT OF SATAN

ISBN 13: 978-1483946351
ISBN 10: 1483946355

Published by
Motivation Basics
P.O. Box 6327
Diamondhead, MS 39525

For more information about the author
visit
AuthorsDen.com

QUOTE

"A nation can survive its fools, and even the ambitious. But it cannot survive treason from within. An enemy at the gates is less formidable, for he is known and carries his banner openly. But the traitor moves amongst those within the gate freely, his sly whispers rustling through all the alleys, heard in the very halls of government itself. For the traitor appears not a traitor; he speaks in accents familiar to his victims, and he wears their face and their arguments, he appeals to the baseness that lies deep in the hearts of all men. He rots the soul of a nation, he works secretly and unknown in the night to undermine the pillars of the city, he infects the body politic so that it can no longer resist. A murderer is less to fear. The traitor is the plague." Marcus Tullius Cicero, 58 B.C. Speech in the Roman Senate

"He that hath an ear, let him hear what the Spirit saith unto the churches; He that overcometh shall not be hurt of the second death.

And to the angel of the church in Pergamos write; These things saith he which hath the sharp sword with two edges;

I know thy works, and where thou dwellest, even where Satan's seat is; and thou holdest fast my name, and hast not denied my faith, even in those days wherein Antipas was my faithful martyr, who was slain among you, where Satan dwelleth."

From the Bible, Book of Revelation Chapter 2, Verses 11-13. Written by Apostle John from the Island of Patmos.

Contents

INTRODUCTION

An article appeared on October 12, 2012, regarding Obama's ring. In that article it was stated that it's the same ring he has worn for many years and is also the ring used when Michelle Obama put it on his finger when they were married. That article suggested the ring had an engraving of part of the Shahada, the Islamic declaration that 'There is no god except Allah, and Mohammed is the messenger of Allah.'

Allegedly, according to that article, only the first half of the Shahada was engraved on the ring. The photograph of the ring had such low resolution it was not really clear what was engraved. Even experts asked to examine the photographs could not confirm that was the engraving. That allegation was later debunked when it was shown by photographs with better resolution cameras that the engraving was that of coiled serpents, not the Shahada.

That finding presented an even more disturbing scenario than what had been alleged. It made a direct connection to the 'seat of Satan' mentioned in Apostle John's writings to the seven biblical churches of Asia Minor while he was exiled on the island of Patmos. John's indirect reference to the serpent opened doors to discovering other connections between Satan and the serpent, often identified as the dragon or the beast in other areas of the Bible. The identifications of these names is often confusing and will be interpreted in other sections of this book. Generally, however, the serpent and the dragon, called in some places, 'that old dragon' refers to the devil. He's referred to as the devil or Satan - or 'that old dragon.'

References to the beast and the antichrist describe a different entity. And, the reference to the plural 'antichrists' is even different. There have been, and will be more antichrists. Only one antichrist is described throughout the Bible as the 'beast.' The other antichrists describe themselves, or are seen by others, as Jesus, the Messiah.

The most dangerous antichrist, the beast, will not assign himself to that role. Satan will choose him and assign him those great powers when Satan chooses. Now that person does not know he will become the End Times antichrist. This is according to Revelation, Chapter 13, the first two verses:

> "And I stood upon the sand of the sea, and saw a beast rise up out of the sea, having seven heads and ten horns, and upon his horns ten crowns, and upon his heads the name of blasphemy.
>
> 2 And the beast which I saw was like unto a leopard, and his feet were as the feet of a bear, and his mouth as the mouth of a lion: and the dragon gave him his power, and his seat, and great authority."

At this time, that person is building his power base thinking he's doing great things for mankind. He will get his full power, and that assignment to be that beast, that antichirst, when the seven continents, the seven heads, are combined under one rule.

Chapter 1

THE SERPENT RING

How and why is the reference to John's writing to the church at Pergamos relevant? Although it's a short excerpt from the Bible, it contains many concepts. John wrote to the seven biblical churches from the island of Patmos where he was exiled by Emperor Domitian for his religious teachings throughout Asia Minor, but mainly in Ephesus.

Patmos is an island six miles off the coast of Turkey that still bears that name, near what was the church of Ephesus. The current name of the city near the ruins of Ephesus is Seljuk.

John was released from exile when Domitian was assassinated, in 96 CE, and returned to Ephesus where he remained free until his death. He was thought to be at least a hundred years old when he died. It's also believed he wrote his Gospel there after he was released from exile.

How important was Ephesus, and what was John doing there? It was the capital of Rome's Asia Province and also the site of the Temple of Diana, one of the Seven Wonders of the ancient world. The worship of Diana was one of the problems facing the Christians in Ephesus while Paul and then John taught there. Christians were ridiculed and outcast because their religion complicated the livelihood of many local silversmiths. Silversmiths made their living by selling replicas of the goddess Diana. Paul's preaching included the proclamation that, "There are no Gods made with hands."

Ephesus is important for other reasons. It's also where John brought Mary, approximately forty years later, after his promise to Jesus that he would take care of her. She is thought to have remained there until she died. It's believed the foundation of her last home sits high above Ephesus, now Seljuk, in a large grove of ancient fig trees. The location was discovered through the vision of a German Nun named Catherine Emmerich who never left Germany. The home was rebuilt as a shrine and it still sits, today, on high ground overlooking the vast ruins of the ancient city of Ephesus. In John's letter to the church at Ephesus, he made reference to those fig trees, which suggests he knew the location of Mary's home.

Ephesus also built the first Christian basilica and is the destination of Christians longer than any other site in Christendom. The basilica was built there in the sixth century by Emperor Justinian. The ruins cover an older church built over the tomb of the Apostle John. The name reads, 'Saint Jean's Basilica.' The second Ecumenical Council was held there in 431 where Mary was proclaimed the Blessed Mother.

While John was exiled to Patmos, supposedly because of his advanced age, two other followers of Jesus were not so lucky as John. Paul of Tarsus, originally a Roman citizen named Saul, and Timothy were sent to Rome. Paul was beheaded since he was a Roman citizen and couldn't be crucified on a cross. Timothy, a Jew, was crucified upside down in Rome.

While Paul and Timothy were in Rome, John wrote letters to the seven churches which were nearby in Turkey. All were important, but probably none as clear and specific as the one he sent to Pergamos. His letters in the Book of Revelation also referred to angels and candlesticks. In that scripture he described angels as the church leaders and candlesticks as the churches. He began the letter to Pergamos:

> "He that hath an ear, let him hear what the Spirit saith unto the churches; He that overcometh shall not be hurt of the second death."

Later, in Revelation, Chapter 20, John explains his vision further concerning the second death in verses 12-15.

> "And I saw the dead, small and great, stand before God; and the books were opened; and another book was opened, which is the book of life; and the dead were judged out of those things which were written in the books, according to their works.
> And the sea gave up the dead which were in it; and death and hell delivered up the dead which were in them: and they were judged every man according to their works.
> And death and hell were cast into the lake of fire. This is the second death. And whosoever was not found written in the book of life was cast into the lake of fire."

From this information, the reference to the second death in John's letter to Pergamos seems rather clear. It means those who hold fast to their Christian faith should not fear the second death. That's the day of judgement when all souls will be judged according to their works. The reference to the sea may be somewhat misleading until further readings reveal that the sea, in many references in the Bible, refers to the sea of mankind, or the sea of souls. This does not mean from a large body of water. This calls to question - when will this day of judgement occur?

Actually, according to several verses in Chapter 20 of Revelation there will be two judgements, or resurrections. This is often confusing because of the placement of words.

Verse 4 says the souls of those who are beheaded by the beast because they had not worshiped him or his image, or had not received his mark upon their foreheads or in their hands would live and reign with Christ a thousand years. This is after the beast and the false prophet are both "cast alive into a lake of fire burning with brimstone." The souls of those who are killed for refusing to worship the beast are resurrected first.

Verse 5 creates some confusion because it states, "But the rest of the dead lived not again until the thousand years were finished. This is the first resurrection." This last sentence seems misplaced and perhaps should have been at the end of Verse 4.

If my interpretation is correct, the second resurrection occurs after the devil is dealt with at the end of the thousand years. This is in Verse 10, which reads:

> "And the devil that deceived them was cast into the lake of fire and brimstone, where the beast and the false prophet are, and shall be tormented day and night for ever and ever."

> Verse 12, stated earlier, reads, "And I saw the dead, small and great, stand before God; and the books were opened, which is the book of life; and the dead were judged out of those things which were written in the books, according to

their works."

These words in this sequence describe the two resurrections. The first is for those who stood firm in their belief in Jesus and refused to worship the beast (the 666 beast- the antichrist) and were beheaded for doing so. The second resurrection is for all others throughout time - except possibly those called to be angels or saints for messages or missions. In many cases the word 'angel' is used to refer to a messenger, which could be either earthly or heavenly.

The second part of the reference, Chapter 2, Verse 12, used a more cryptic word, 'sword.' It's obviously a reference to the multiple powers of Jesus, but one may only guess at those powers.

"And to the angel of the church in Pergamos write; These things saith he which hath the sharp sword with two edges;"

Other references in the Bible use the sword allegory in reference to the power of voice or speech. Perhaps that's the case with this reference to one edge of the sword. Perhaps the other edge is the power to judge, as from names written in the 'book of life.' This is only a guess on my part. Perhaps others more learned in Bible verse will have more appropriate interpretations.

Chapter 2: Verse 13, is perhaps the most revealing comment in the Bible. Although stated in a short verse, and only to the church at Pergamos, it gives clear visibility and definition to the difference in good and evil, and truth and deceit. It states:

"I know they works, and where thou dwellest, even where Satan's seat is; and thou holdest

> fast my name, and hast not denied my faith,
> even in those days wherein Antipas was my
> faithful martyr, who was slain among you,
> where Satan dwelleth."

Before we decipher the comment about 'Satan's seat,' let's first understand the role of Antipas. Antipas was thought to be one of Jesus's first disciples. He was also a bishop at Pergamum (Pergamos) and never wavered from Christ's word, as stated above, "hast not denied my faith." He is believed to have been put to death by Emperor Domitian, the same emperor who exiled John to Patmos. Reportedly, he was killed by being burned inside a brazen (brass) bull. Others also killed in that same manner were Agathonice, Carpus, Polybus and Attalus. Attalus likely was from the Attalid dynasty that bequeathed Pergamum to Rome.

These deaths were prompted by priests from the cult of Aesculapius. The icon for Aesculapius was the serpent. The serpent represents the devil and evil throughout the Bible. Hence, "where Satan dwelleth and the seat of Satan."

So, how did the serpent come to represent the devil, Satan, to be 'Satan's seat' in Pergamum, often pronounced Pergamos? It was established by an Attalus prince. During the Attalid dynasty from 214-133 B.C., Prince Archias went to the Temple of Aesculapius in Epidaurus, Greece to recover from battle wounds. He was so grateful for his recovery that he brought several doctor-priests back to Pergamum and established the Asklepieion there. Aesculapius was the god of medicine and the serpent and staff were his symbol, his icon.

The ruins of the Temple of Aesculapius are still adorned with carvings of the serpent. Serpents were also used in dark tunnels to perform certain healing rites at the Temple of Telesporos. Telesporos was considered the god of cure-revealing dreams. It also had healing fountains in the courtyard used by many known leaders of the ancient world.

In 133 B.C. the last king, Attalus III, died and

bequeathed his kingdom to Rome. In the Roman era, both Marcus Aurelius and Caracalla went there to be healed.

Barack Obama's prized wedding ring which he has worn for many years, even before he was married, holds two coiled serpent icons. Obviously, he treasures the serpents' relevance on his ring as did the ancients in Pergamum who worshiped their serpent icon. Furthermore, that 'old serpent' is mentioned many times in the Bible as the deceiver who tries to lead people from the words of God. According to the Bible the first encounter with that deceiving serpent was in the beginning.

Mankind's first encounter with the serpent was when he met Eve, the first woman, in the Garden of Eden. And what did the old serpent do? His first act was to deceive Eve about the fruit of the tree in the midst of the garden. This encounter is described in Genesis, Chapter 3:

> "Now the serpent was more subtil than any beast of the field which the Lord God had made. And he said unto the woman, Yea, hath God said, Ye shall not eat of every tree of the garden?
> 2 And the woman said unto the serpent, We may eat of the fruit of the trees of the garden:
> 3 But of the fruit of the tree which is in th midst of the garden, God hath said, Ye shall not eat of it, neither shall ye touch it, lest ye die.
> 4 And the serpent said unto the woman, Ye shall not surely die:
> 5 For God doth know that in the day ye eat thereof, then your eyes shall be opened, and ye shall be as gods, knowing good and evil."

The rest of that story is common history. Eve ate the fruit, supposedly the apple, then gave some to Adam. Their eyes became open and they were aware of right and wrong and evil and good. God sent them from the Garden of Eden to toil the rest of their lives. And, mankind was assigned to toil forever. The serpent was assigned to crawl on his belly in the dust forever.

That story in Genesis was a long time ago. No one really knows how old. During that long time the climate has changed and shifted on the face of the earth; where rivers once flowed at the Garden of Eden, now harsh dry land prevails; major kings and dynasties have come and gone; and politics on the globe keep shifting always in favor of those who control the most power.

Often that power is determined not necessarily by strength alone, but often by deception, that same deception created by Satan in the Garden of Eden. That old serpent is as alive today as he was in the Garden of Eden. He takes many forms and shapes, but his actions and words are still those of the serpent who turned mankind against the words of God. Although the serpent is Satan's first known visible form of deceit, it takes many forms as proclaimed by Second John 1:7:

"For many deceivers are entered into the world,
who confess not that Jesus Christ is come in
the flesh. This is a deceiver and an antichrist."

Does Barack Obama follow his serpents, the seat of Satan, to also deceive American citizens? Will he deceive even more in the future? Before we consider some of Obama's deceptions let's first look at some of those deceptions described in the Bible. These deceptions refer to those of the many antichrists.

Yes, there were, and still are many antichrists. These are the deceivers who either attempt to take the place of Jesus, or who are assumed by their followers to be the Messiah, or even God the Almighty. A later chapter will explain how Barack Obama follows their characteristics.

Chapter 2

MANY ANTICHRISTS

According to Apostle John there will be many deceivers, and obviously for many purposes. As described in the Genesis story about Adam and Eve the purpose of the serpent, who was Satan in disguise, was to turn Adam and Eve against the plan God had for them. But, this reference goes further and has broader implications, especially regarding the definition of the antichrist. In modern times the reference is generally 'the antichrist.' Since this idea that the antichrist is only one, many have not been identified as one of the antichrists, in the past. This is what First John 2:18 in the Bible says:

> "Little children, it is the last time; and as ye have heard that Antichrist shall come, even now are there many Antichrists; whereby we know that it is the last time."

19

Here John says there are many antichrists, then he asks the question, do we know if the current one is the last one. Throughout history, we have asked the question if someone of that time is the antichrist. After they pass and Armageddon doesn't occur, then we say, "That must not have been the antichrist." Adolph Hitler probably is the best modern example of this concept. Was Hitler 'the' antichrist? No. Was Hitler 'an' antichrist? Yes.

Although he never claimed to be Jesus or God, as Christians understand God, he began his reign of terror by claiming to be on the side of goodness and right to reclaim the greater glory that once was the 'Fatherland.' His actions and great speeches began by promising to return defeated Germany back to its prestige position before it was defeated and humiliated in World War I. He deceived German citizens; they believed him; then Germany was moved to the side of evil.

Satan controlled them through his presence in the body of a man named Adolph Hitler. To his faithful followers he was their god, leading them back to their promised land - their position of power they occupied before.

Understanding the definition of antichrist that it is not someone who proclaims 'against' Jesus, but instead acts in the place of or claims to be Jesus - and eventually God. The last antichrist will sit on the throne in Jerusalem in the last days, during the abomination of desolation, and claim to be God. Is it possible that many American citizens who are considered rational and sane can be convinced, or convince themselves, even today that they are in the presence of the Messiah, the returned Jesus? We have many current examples. And when the crisis is passed others ask how that could happen. They ask how those followers could be that stupid and irrational.

Three recent examples come to mind. The first is the saga of Jim Jones of Jonestown fame. Another is David Koresh and the Dividians. William Branham was one of the first modern ones. He was the father of faith healing who helped Jim Jones get his start.

Jim Jones
(May 1931 - November 1978)

Who was the popular Jim Jones? Where did he come from? What did he do? Did his beginnings indicate or suggest his climatic evil? The following information about Jim Jones is extracted from Wikipedia. Some information could be imperfect, but none presented here has been discounted in any other parts of Wikipedia itself. References given within Wikipedia refer to other reliable sources.

James Warren (Jim) Jones was born in Indiana on May 13, 1931 to James Thurman Jones and Lynetta Putnam Jones. When Jim was born his mother Lynetta professed that she had given birth to a messiah. He grew up with his poor family near Lynn, Indiana in a shack without plumbing where they had moved because of conditions during the depression. According to friends, he was a rather weird child often holding funerals for small animals, possibly some he even killed himself for that purpose. It was suspected that his father was a member of the Ku Klux Klan during that time.

When his parents separated, he moved with his mother to Richmond, Indiana and graduated with honors from high school there in 1948. During his time in school he was a good student and an avid reader. Much of his reading was the study of works regarding Adolph Hitler, Mahatma Gandhi, Joseph Stalin, and Karl Marx. He married a nurse named Marceline Baldwin after he graduated high school and moved to Bloomington, Indiana. While attending Indiana University there where he was impressed with a speech by Eleanor Roosevelt regarding the plight of blacks in America. Jim and Marceline moved to Indianapolis in 1951, where he attended night school at Butler University earning a degree in secondary education years later, 1961.

He moved toward a Communist ideology when he moved to Indianapolis, often attending Communist meetings and rallies. He seemed especially disturbed from events of the McCarthy Hearings at that time, which exposed many Communist theories and rumors. Even his mother was scrutinized by authorities after attending some meetings, particularly one conducted by a suspected Communist of that time named Paul Robeson.

(Paul Robeson was a famous African-American athlete, singer, actor, and advocate for the civil rights of people around the world. He rose to prominence in a time when segregation was legal in the United States, and black people were being lynched by racist mobs, especially in the South. He was accused by the House Un-American Activities Committee as being a Communist. More about Robeson is detailed in his autobiography titled, 'Here I Stand.')

Jones expressed frustration with all the open ostracism of Communists at that time and decided to develop his Marxism by infiltrating the church. Although known to be a Communist at that time, he became a student pastor at a Methodist Church, in Indianapolis, in 1952. He soon left that church when he claimed the church barred him from integrating Blacks into his congregation. He was anxious to form his own church but lacked the necessary funds.

He found the source of funds when he witnessed the attraction of people to a faith-healing service by the Seventh Day Baptist Church. He organized a large religious convention for June 11-15, 1956, and arranged to share the convention with Reverend William M. Branham, a minister of very high standing at that time. His name was as recognizable as that of Oral Roberts and Billy Graham. (A brief review of Branham's background reveals he also believed he was a special prophet called by angels he saw in visions to become a prophetic religious leader.) Jones moved away from his openly Communist stand when the Communist Party USA became concerned about actions and policies by the Soviet leader, Joseph Stalin.

Jones was appointed director of the Human Rights Commission in 1960 by Indianapolis Democratic Mayor Charles Boswell. Although advised to keep a lower profile in that position, Jones ignored it and became even more outspoken on local radio and television programs supporting the NAACP and Urban League, even at one meeting shouting, "Let my people go!" as he urged them to become even more militant. He was involved in many other integration projects at that time. Many incidents occurred against Jones at that time for his integration views, some he was believed to have been involved with himself to create more outrage and support for himself at that time.

After Jones formed his 'Peoples Temple,' he visited Brazil, in 1965 then returned and claimed the world would be engulfed in a nuclear way on July 15, 1967, that would create a new socialist Eden on earth. He decided to move the Peoples Temple to Redwood Valley, California which he considered a safer place. He continued to speak of the social gospel's virtues, without admitting he actually held communist feelings. Eventually he began teaching his 'Apostolic' Socialism in his temples. His teachings included those such as, "If you're born in capitalist America, racist America, fascist America, then you're born in sin. But if you're born in socialism, you're not born in sin."

He also began preaching that he was the reincarnation of Mahatma Gandhi, Father Divine, as well as Jesus of Nazareth, Buddha, and Vladimir Lenin. In the documentary 'Jonestown: The Life and Death of Peoples Temple,' former Temple member Hue Fortson, Jr. quoted Jones as saying, "What you need to believe in is what you can see ... If you see me as your friend, I'll be your friend. As you see me as your father, I'll be your father, for those of you that don't have a father ... If you see me as your savior, I'll be your savior. If you see me as your God, I'll be your God."

Marceline Jones admitted to the New York Times that, as early as age 18 when he watched his then idol Mao Zedong overthrow the Chinese government, Jim Jones realized that the way to achieve social change through Marxism in the United States was to mobilize people through religion. "Jim used religion to try to get some people out of the opiate of religion," and had slammed the Bible on the table yelling "I've got to destroy this paper idol!" In one sermon, Jones said that, "You're gonna help yourself, or you'll get no help! There's only one hope of glory; that's within you! Nobody's gonna come out of the sky! There's no heaven up there! We'll have to make heaven down here!"

The move of Peoples Temple headquarters to San Francisco in 1975 invigorated Jones' political career. After the Temple served an important role in the mayoral election victory of George Moscone in 1975, Moscone appointed Jones as the chairman of the San Francisco Housing Authority Commission. In that position he advanced his status and political position. For example, he had respected contact with vice presidential candidate Walter Mondale on his campaign plane, where Mondale praised the work of the Temple. He also met with Rosalyn Carter several times, discussing Cuba among other topics of current political interest. They also spoke together at the San Francisco Democratic Party Headquarters grand opening, where Jones got more applause than did the First Lady.

In September 1977, Willie Brown served as master of ceremonies at a large testimonial dinner for Jones attended by Governor Jerry Brown and Lieutenant Governor Mervyn Dymally and other political figures. At that dinner, while introducing Jones, Willie Brown is reported to have said "Let me present to you what you should see every day when you look in the mirror in the early morning hours.... Let me present to you a combination of Martin King, Angela Davis,

Albert Einstein, and Chairman Mao."

Although his move to San Francisco brought Jones much attention and more association with influential political leaders it also opened him to more scrutiny. In the summer of 1977, Jones and several hundred Temple members moved to the Temple's "Agricultural Project" in Guyana after they learned of the contents of a reporter's article to be published in which former Temple members claimed they were physically, emotionally, and sexually abused. Jones named the settlement Jonestown after himself.

Jones had first started building Jonestown in 1970 as a means to create both a "socialist paradise" and a "sanctuary" from the media scrutiny which had started in 1972. Here they also established a cooperative called the "People's Temple Agricultural Project." Regarding the former goal, Jones purported to establish Jonestown as a benevolent model communist community stating, "I believe we're the purest communists there are." In that regard, like the restrictive emigration policies of the then Soviet Union, Cuba, North Korea, and other communist states, Jones did not permit members to leave Jonestown.

Even with the allegations before Jones left for Jonestown, he is still respected by some for setting up a racially mixed church which helped the disadvantaged. Approximately 68 percent of Jonestown's residents were black. Jonestown is also the place where Jones began his belief called "Translation" where he and his followers would all die together and move to another planet and live blissfully.

On April 11, 1978, concerned relatives of some members in Jonestown distributed a packet of documents, including letters and affidavits titled an "Accusation of Human Rights Violations by Rev. James Warren Jones" to the Peoples Temple, members of the press and members of Congress. In June 1978, escaped Temple member Deborah Layton provided the group with a further affidavit detailing alleged crimes by the Peoples Temple and substandard living conditions in Jonestown.

Facing increasing scrutiny, in the summer of 1978, Jones also hired noted JFK assassination conspiracy theorists Mark Lane and Donald Freed to help make the case of a "grand conspiracy" by intelligence agencies against the Peoples Temple. Jones told Lane he wanted to "pull an Eldridge Cleaver," referring to a fugitive Black Panther who was able to return to the United States after repairing his reputation.

In November, 1978, U.S. Congressman Leo Ryan led a fact-finding mission to Jonestown to investigate allegations of human rights abuses. Ryan's delegation included relatives of Temple members Don Harris, an NBC network news reporter, an NBC cameraman and reporters for various newspapers. On November 17, Ryan's delegation traveled by airplane to Jonestown. The delegation left hurriedly the afternoon of November 18 after Temple member Don Sly attacked Ryan with a knife. The attack was thwarted, bringing the visit to an abrupt end. Congressman Ryan and his people succeeded in taking with them fifteen People's Temple members who had expressed a wish to leave. At that time, Jones made no attempt to prevent their departure.

As members of Ryan's delegation boarded two planes at the airstrip, Jones' Red Brigade armed guards arrived in a tractor-pulled trailer and began shooting at the delegation. The guards killed Congressman Ryan and four others at the airstrip.

Later that same day, 909 inhabitants of Jonestown, 303 of them children, died of apparent cyanide poisoning, mostly in and around a pavilion. This resulted in the greatest single loss of American civilian life in a non-natural disaster until the September 11, 2001 attacks. No video was taken during the mass suicide, though the FBI did recover a 45 minute audio recording of the suicide in progress.

On that tape, Jones tells Temple members that the Soviet Union, with whom the Temple had been negotiating a potential exodus for months, would not take them after the Temple had murdered Ryan and four others at a nearby airstrip. The reason given by Jones to commit suicide was consistent with his previously stated conspiracy theories of intelligence organizations allegedly conspiring against the Temple.

Jones was found dead in a deck chair with a gunshot wound to his head that Guyanese coroner Cyrill Mootoo stated was consistent with a self-inflicted gun wound. However, Jones' son Stephan believes his father may have directed someone else to shoot him

William M. Branham
(1909-1965)

William Marrion Branham was a Christian minister usually credited with founding the post WWII divine healing movement. While many Pentecostal Christians welcomed his evangelistic and healing ministry, and some considered him to be a prophet, a minority have given him an even higher status, believing that his ministry and teachings were supernaturally vindicated by God. Some observers refer to this as 'Branhamism.' His closest followers prefer the name 'Message Believers.' He taught that believers should return to the original apostolic faith of the Bible that according to Hebrews 13:8 "Jesus Christ the same yesterday, and today, and for ever."

Branham was born in a log cabin in Cumberland County, Kentucky in a casually-devout Roman Catholic family. His father was a logger and an alcoholic. He claimed that from his early childhood he had supernatural experiences including prophetic visions. He claimed that in his early childhood, while getting water from a creek, he heard the voice of the Angel of the Lord who told him 'never to drink, smoke, or defile his body, for there would be work for him when he got older.'

Leaving home at 19, he worked on a ranch in Arizona and also claiming to have had a short career as a boxer, winning 15 fights in Golden Gloves. At 22 he said he had a conversion experience and was later ordained as an assistant pastor at a Missionary Baptist Church. When he disagreed with the pastor about the role of women preaching, he held a series of revivals on his own in a tent. He later held meetings at a Masonic temple until his group could construct a building, in 1933. The congregation named the building Branham Tabernacle.

History suggests his healing campaigns started as early as 1941. In 1946 he claimed to have an angelic visitation to start his worldwide ministry of evangelism and faith healing. His first meetings as a full-time evangelist were held in St. Louis in June, 1946. A professor from the University of Birmingham supposedly wrote, "Branham's sensational healing services, which began in 1946, are well documented and he was the pacesetter for those who followed." Other notables have commented, "Historians generally mark this turn in Branham's ministry as inaugurating the modern healing revival."

Branham said that his evangelistic healing ministry started one night during his search for personal meaning. He claimed that in May, 1946, an angel in the form of a man appeared, saying, "Do not fear. I am sent from the presence of the Almighty God to tell you that your particular birth and misunderstood life has been to indicate that you are to take a gift of Divine healing to the peoples of the world."

The most unexplained occurrence with Branham involved a circle of light, resembling a halo, exposed by a photograph taken while he was standing at a podium having a debate. The negative was investigated and never proven to be fraudulent. Branham believed the light was supernatural and was a verification of his ministry. According to this Wikipedia article, a copy of the photograph is held in the

Library of Congress photograph collection.

According to Branham a cluster of seven angels met him on Sunset Mountain (Peak) northeast of Tucson, Arizona, in the Galiuro Mountains to commission the revealing of the 'Seven Seals' described in the Book of Revelation. A cloud formation resembling the head of Christ had appeared over Flagstaff a few days earlier. He claimed this was a sign vindicating the vision he revealed earlier to his congregation regarding the Seven Seals. He claimed the cloud was formed by the same angels who met him at Sunset Mountain.

Branham was killed with members of his family in an automobile accident near Friona, Texas, on December 18, 1965. He died on December 24. It was reported in the press that some of his followers predicted he would return to life during Easter, but his family members said Branham never taught this.

David Koresh
(August 1959 - April 1993)

David Koresh is another modern-day antichrist. His activities had the same disastrous results as did Jim Jones.

Who was David Koresh? The answer also comes from information presented in Wikipedia. This information has not been verified but is presented as offered.

David Koresh's mother was a 14-year-old unmarried girl named Bonnie Sue Clark. His father was a 20-year-old named Bobby Howell. Howell abandoned David's mother even before David was born. David never met his father. David was born on August 17, 1959 and given the name Vernon Wayne Howell. After Howell abandoned Bonnie Sue, she lived with another boyfriend. When she separated from that boyfriend she left David (Vernon Wayne) with his maternal grandmother when he was 4 years old. Bonnie Sue later married and reclaimed David when he was 7 years old.

He wasn't a good student in school, suffering from poor study skills and dyslexia, and was assigned to a Special Education class. He was nicknamed 'Mister Retardo' by his classmates. He dropped out of school in his junior year at Garland, Texas High School. He impregnated a 15-year-old girl with whom he had an affair when he was 22.

He later claimed to be a born-again Christian in the Southern Baptist Church. He later joined his mother's Seventh-day Adventist Church where he fell in love with the pastor's young daughter. He tried to convince the pastor that it was God's will that he have his young daughter for his wife. He became so persistent that he was finally expelled from the church.

He moved to Waco, Texas in 1981 where he joined the Branch Davidians, a religious group formed as a separation in the 1950s from the 'Shepard's Rod.' The Shepard's Rod group had separated themselves as a branch of the Seventh-day Adventist Church in the 1930s. Headquarters for this group was located ten miles from Waco, on a ranch they called, The Mount Carmel Center. While there he played guitar and sang at church services. It's also reported that he and his rock band played at clubs in Waco, and that he even tried to form his own record company to produce his own music. That endeavor failed, supposedly for lack of funds.

In 1983 he began claiming he had the gift of prophecy. The Dividian leader and prophetess, Lois Roden, began allowing him to teach his own message in the organization. It's reported that although she was 76 years old she claimed that God had chosen him to father a child with her, who would be the Chosen One. This caused a controversy with her son, George Roden, who intended to be the group's next leader. The tension eased when Koresh announced that God had instructed him to marry another woman named Rachel Jones. She was already using Koresh's last name. After a short period of calm the power struggle for control of the group returned. At this point, George Roden forced Koresh and his group off the property at gunpoint. Another splinter group of the Dividians voluntarily left at the same time.

Koresh and his small group moved to Palestine, Texas where they lived in camp-like conditions another two years. During that time, he sought followers in California, the United Kingdom, Israel and Australia. He also visited Israel, where he claimed to have a vision that he was the modern-day Cyrus the Great, the founder of the Dividian movement. Convinced that his destiny was to reestablish the Dividian movement in Israel, he finally decided it would be at the location of the Dividians at Mount Carmel near Waco.

After a long series of unusual activities such as a challenge to raise corpses to life between George Roden and Koresh, and the murder by George Roden with an ax of another man who claimed to be the Messiah, Koresh and his followers gained control of Mount Carmel by paying unpaid taxes on the property. Many of the Dividians still on the property had already turned to Koresh as their leader even before Roden was jailed for the murder of Wayman Adair who claimed to be the Messiah. Roden was jailed in a mental institution.

Vernon Howell (Koresh) petitioned a California court on May 15, 1990 to legally change his name to 'David Koresh.' His petition was granted on August 28, 1990. He chose the name 'David' to show his direct lineage to King David of the Bible. He chose the name 'Koresh' which is a transliteration of the Persian name of King Cyrus. With this name he was professing himself to be the spiritual descendent of King David who was carrying out a biblical quest similar to King Cyrus of Persia.

Koresh and his followers remained at the Mount Carmel location near Waco until the end, which is recent history. His life ended, along with 54 other adults and 28 children on April 19, 1993 when the building in which they had confined themselves in the 51-day standoff ended with the assault by U.S. authorities. The building caught fire, or was set fire, and all those inside perished. Thus ended the life and history of another antichrist.

The reason for the Mount Carmel assault remains a mystery. Some conspiracy theorists claim Israel was involved, since Koresh had come to Israel claiming to be Jesus. Questions about the event eventually disappeared without any clear answers from the government.

Chapter 3

OTHER ANTICHRISTS

As First John 2:18 says, "There are many antichrists." The following are just a few of the many others that can be found with enough research. Some are recent enough to still be remembered. Others are from other cultures and times. As a reminder, it's not necessary they openly claim to be Jesus Christ, the returned Messiah, or God; only that they deny others who make that claim of them or treat them as such. We will begin with another recent one that should be well remembered.

Marshall Herff Applewhite, Jr.
(May 17, 1931 - March 1997)

We can't forget one of our more recent ones who led his people to plan for a space flight to Heaven on a comet. Applewhite was an American religious person who founded what became known as the Heaven's Gate religious group and organized their mass suicide in 1997. It was the largest mass suicide to occur inside the United States.

Applewhite was a native Texan who attended several universities and then served in the U.S. Army. After finishing school he taught music at the University of Alabama. He later returned to Texas where he served in the music department at the University of St. Thomas, in Houston. He later met Bonnie Nettles, a nurse, and together they decided they were called to be divine messengers. In their early efforts they gained only one convert. He developed his new theology while serving in jail for not returning a rental car.

After his release he went to California and Oregon with Nettles. They eventually gained a group of followers. He initially stated that he and his followers would be visited by extraterrestrials that would give them new bodies with which they would ascend to a spaceship where their bodies would be transformed. He changed that ideology to say their bodies were merely containers of their souls which would be placed into new bodies. His partner, Nettles, died in 1985.

In the 1990s the group took more steps to publicize their theology. In 1996, they learned of the approach of Comet Hale-Bopp and rumors of an accompanying spaceship. They concluded that was the spaceship they were waiting for. They committed suicide in their mansion believing their souls would ascend to the spaceship where they would be given new bodies.

How could this happen? Some commentators attributed his followers' willingness to commit suicide to his skill as a manipulator. Others argued their willingness was due to their faith in the narrative he constructed. Others speculate that Applewhite had brainwashed his followers. This idea was rejected by many academics. Others suggest they followed him to suicide because they had become totally dependent on him and were poorly suited for life in his absence. Another said he accomplished that complete obedience of his followers by isolating them socially and cultivated an attitude of complete obedience to him.

Most of the dead had been with him about 20 years. There were 21 women and 18 men who committed suicide with Applewhite.

The great lesson learned from Applewhite and the Heaven's Gate experience is how rational and sane people can become so devoted to one person they can do irrational things in response to an accepted ideology, or in response to such dependence on one person. Perhaps this is a great example of what's happening to America, even today - especially today.

John Nichols Thom
(1799-1838)

A Cornish tax rebel, Thom claimed to be the 'saviour of the world' and the reincarnation of Jesus Christ and his body temple of the Holy Ghost in 1834. He was killed by British soldiers at the Battle of Bossenden Wood, on May 21, 1838 in Kent, England. When he was a child his mother died in an insane asylum.

He began his odd behavior when he moved to Canterbury and introduced himself as Count Moses R. Rothschild, of the Jewish family Rothschild. A few weeks later he changed his title and his persona to Sir William Percy Honeywood Courtenay, Knight of Malta. In the parliamentary election of 1832, claiming to be the Earl of Devon he won many votes compared to his competitors. He ran as an anti-tax candidate. In 1833 he published a theological journal, 'The Lion,' in which he claimed that all the churches wanted to do was just hoard all the gold. In that same year he also made a false claim against a group of alcohol smugglers, for which he was sentenced for perjury. He was locked up in an insane asylum in Kent.

Later, still under the name of Sir William Courtney, Thom declared himself 'saviour of the world' and became a wandering preacher dressed in colorful costumes, including a Maltese Cross and a sword he claimed to be Excalibur. Witnesses also said that he often showed nail marks in his hands.

Supporting the cause of farm workers who resisted restrictive laws of that time he eventually gathered a following of more than a hundred people. He convinced them that their faith would make them invulnerable to steel and bullets. He also claimed that he could slay thousands of adversaries by hitting his left hand against his right hand. He also proclaimed that if he were shot dead he would come back to life in three days. He created such a rift between farm owners and their workers that the owners brought charges against him. In an attempt to arrest Thom, he killed one of the officers and dismembered his body.

When soldiers went to the village of Dunkirk to arrest Thom and his followers a gunfight resulted in the Bossenden Wood, which became the name of the battle. Two officers were killed along with Thom and nine of his followers. Before his burial, Thom's coroner removed Thom's heart and put in a pickle jar, having heard the rumor that Thom would rise on the third day. The pickled heart survived until the 1950s. Watchmen guarded his grave for some time to prevent grave robbers from claiming he had risen.

Arnold Potter
(January 11, 1804 - April 2, 1872)

Potter was a self-declared Messiah and a leader of a schismatic sect in the Latter Day Saints movement. He claimed the spirit of Jesus Christ entered into his body and he called himself Potter Christ, Son of the living God. He died in an attempt to 'ascend into Heaven' by jumping off a cliff. His body was later retrieved and buried by his followers.

Potter was born in New York. At age 19 he married

Almira Smith. With his wife and children, he moved to Indiana around 1845. He and his family were baptized by missionaries of the Church of Jesus Christ of the Latter Day Saints. He later was given a priesthood by Joseph Smith, Jr. He was later given a patriarchal blessing from church patriarch Joseph Smith, Sr. He later settled in Sand Prairie, Iowa, where he was the presiding elder of the church.

In 1848 he traveled to the Salt Lake Valley as a Mormon pioneer. By 1856, he had moved from Utah Territory to San Bernardino, California. On March 16, 1856 he got a call to serve as a missionary in Australia from LDS Church president, Brigham Young. Later that year he left California for Australia.

He claimed that during his trip to Australia, he underwent a purifying, quickening change whereby the spirit of Jesus Christ entered into his body and he became 'Potter Christ, Son of the living God.' During his time in Australia he wrote a book which he said was dictated to him by angels. It was described by Potter as the book from which all people were to be judged in the Final Judgement.

He returned from Australia and by 1861 he and some of his followers had left California planning to settle near Independence, Missouri, the traditional location of Zion for the Latter Day Saints. They settled at Saint Marys in northwest Mills County, Iowa. When Saint Marys was destroyed by flooding in 1865, they moved to Council Bluffs. Potter spent his days wandering the streets in Council Bluffs wearing a long white robe and became a local oddity.

His followers in Council Bluffs were described as 'few but devout.' The men wore black robes and the women had different grooming practices. Potter and his followers held loud prayer meetings which would often end with him declaring a new revelation from God.

At a church meeting in 1872, Potter announced the time had come for his ascent to Heaven. His disciples followed as he rode a donkey to the edge of the bluffs then leapt off the edge. He died in his attempt to ascend to Heaven. His followers buried his body after his futile attempt.

William W. Davis
(1833-1906)

Davis was a leader of a Latter Day Saint schismatic group called the Kingdom of Heaven, which was located near Walla Walla, Washington from 1867 to 1881. He was born in Wales to a Methodist family and in 1847 converted to Mormonism, and in 1854 he emigrated to the Utah Territory. He became disillusioned with the leadership of the LDS Church after the Mountain Meadows massacre and he turned to Church of the Firstborn (Morrisite) Joseph Morris.

He moved with other Morrisites to Montana, and while there had a series of revelations which instructed him to establish the Kingdom of Heaven near Walla Walla, Washington. He and forty of his followers moved there in 1866 and established a communal society on 80 acres of land of which he held title. His main departure from mainstream Mormonism was his teaching of reincarnation.

Davis taught his group, most coming from California and Portland, Oregon, that he was the reincarnation of the Archangel Michael, and had also lived previous lives as Adam and Abraham, from the Bible. When his first son, Arthur, was born in 1868 he claimed that Arthur was the reincarnated Jesus Christ. Arthur was called 'Walla Walla Jesus' by citizens of the local community.

He declared that his next son, David, was 'God, the Father.' His Kingdom of Heaven began to collapse in 1880, when both his children died of diphtheria. Some of his followers then sued him and won a $3200 judgement. As a result he was forced to sell his property on which his Kingdom existed. That brought an end to his movement as the 'Kingdom of Heaven.' There were 43 members at the time of this breakup. He moved to Mill Creek, Washington and attempted to rebuild his following. Failing to do so, he eventually moved to San Francisco.

Haile Selassie
(1892-1975)

Haile Selassie, Emperor of Ethiopia, did not claim to be Jesus and disapproved of claims that he was Jesus. But the Rastafari movement, which emerged in Jamaica during the 1930s, believes he is the Second Coming. He embodied this when he became Emperor of Ethiopia in 1930, perceived as confirmation of the return of the Messiah in the Book of Revelation in the New Testament, but is also expected to return a second time to initiate the apocalyptic day of judgment. He is also called Jah Ras Tafari, and is often considered to be alive by Rastafari movement members.

Today, Haile Selassie is worshipped as God incarnate among Rastafarians. This name is taken from Haile Selassie's pre-imperial name Ras – meaning Head – a title equivalent to Duke – Tafari Makonnen, which emerged in Jamaica during the 1930s. He is viewed as the Messiah who will lead the peoples of Africa and the African diaspora to freedom. His official titles are Conquering Lion of the Tribe of Judah (Taken from Revalation 5:5.) and King of Kings and Elect of God, and his traditional lineage is thought to be from Solomon and Sheba. Rastafari faith in the incarnate divinity of Haile Selassie began after news reports of his coronation reached Jamaica, particularly from the two Time magazine articles on his coronation the week before and the week after the event.

Haile Selassie's own ideas and proclamations increased the philosophy of the movement. In 1961, the Jamaican government sent a delegation composed of both Rastafari and non-Rastafari leaders to Ethiopia to discuss the matter of repatriation, among other issues, with the emperor. He reportedly told the Rastafarian delegation, which included Mortimer Planno, "Tell the Brethren to be not dismayed, I personally will give my assistance in the matter of repatriation."

Haile Selassie visited Jamaica on 21 April 1966, and approximately one hundred thousand Rastafari from all over Jamaica descended on the airport in Kingston, having heard that the man whom they considered to be their messiah was coming to visit them. Haile Selassie arrived at the airport but was unable to come down the mobile steps of the airplane, as the crowd rushed the tarmac. He then returned into the plane, disappearing for several more minutes. Finally, Jamaican authorities were obliged to request Planno, a well-known Rasta leader, to climb the steps, enter the plane, and negotiate the emperor's descent.

Planno re-emerged and announced to the crowd: "The Emperor has instructed me to tell you to be calm. Step back and let the Emperor land". This day is widely held by scholars to be a major turning point for the movement, and it is still commemorated by Rastafarians as Grounation Day, the anniversary of which is celebrated as the second holiest holiday after 2 November, the emperor's Coronation Day.

From then on, as a result of Planno's actions, the Jamaican authorities were asked to ensure that Rastafarian representatives were present at all state functions attended by the emperor, and Rastafarian elders also ensured that they obtained a private audience with the emperor, where he reportedly told them that they should not emigrate to Ethiopia until they had first liberated the people of Jamaica. This dictum came to be known as 'liberation before repatriation.'

Haile Selassie defied expectations of the Jamaican authorities, and never rebuked the Rastafari for their belief in him as the returned Jesus. Instead, he presented the movement's faithful elders with gold medallions – the only recipients of such an honour on this visit.

During soon-to-be Prime Minister Michael Manley's visit to Ethiopia in October 1969, the emperor allegedly still recalled his 1966 reception with amazement, and stated that he felt that he had to be respectful of their beliefs. This was the visit when Manley received the 'Rod of Correction' or 'Rod of Joshua' as a present from the emperor, which is thought to have helped him win the 1972 election in Jamaica.

Bob Marley's wife, Rita, converted to the Rastafari faith after seeing Haile Selassie on his Jamaican trip. She claimed in interviews that she saw a stigmata print on the palm of Haile Selassie's hand, as he waved to the crowd, which resembled the markings on Christ's hands from being nailed to the cross. This claim was never supported by other sources, but was used as evidence for her and other Rastafarians to suggest that Haile Selassie was indeed their messiah.

When Bob Marley converted to Rastafani, that belief became much better known throughout much of the world. Bob Marley's posthumously released song 'Iron Lion Zion' refers to Haile Selassie.

It's unknown if Selassie himself ever denied his divinity. Former senator and Gleaner editor, Hector Wynter, tells of asking him, during his visit to Jamaica in 1966, when he was going to tell Rastafarians he was not God. "Who am I to disturb their belief?" he replied.

Krishna Venta
(March 29, 1911 - December 10, 1958)

Born Francis Herman Pencovic, he was the American leader of a California religious group. In the late 1940s, Venta founded the 'WKFL' (Wisdom, Knowledge, Faith and Love) Fountain of the World cult in Simi Valley, California.

The Fountain of the World became famous in the press in the 1940s and 1950s for uniformly dressing in robes, going barefoot, and requiring its male members to grow beards and wear their hair long. The Fountain was marginally controversial because one of the requirements for membership was that one donate all worldly assets to the group prior to joining. For most who joined the Fountain, however, this was irrelevant since few had much in the way of possessions anyway.

Activities of the group included fighting wildfires, offering shelter to those in need, and feeding the homeless. The group first gained national exposure in 1949 when the news wires picked up the story that Fountain members had been among the first on the scene to offer aid to the victims of Standard Airlines Flight 897R, which had crashed into the Simi Hills, killing 35 of the 48 persons on board.

Pencovic, who stated in April 1948, "I may as well say it: I am Christ. I am the new messiah," and who claimed to have led a convoy of rocketships to Earth from the extinct planet Neophrates, legally changed his name to "Krishna Venta" in the California Courts in 1951.

He died in Chatsworth, California on December 10, 1958 in a suicide bombing instigated by two disgruntled former followers who, although they never offered any documentary evidence to support their claims, charged that Venta had both mishandled cult funds and been intimate with their wives.

A branch of the WKFL Fountain of the World cult was also established in Homer, Alaska in the years prior to Venta's death. Fountain membership at both sites declined rapidly following Venta's death, and the cult had ceased to exist entirely by the mid-1970s.

Sun Myung Moon
(1920-2012)

Moon was believed by members of his Unification Church to be the Messiah and the Second Coming of Christ, fulfilling Jesus' unfinished mission. Dedicated members of the church, Unificationists, consider Moon and his wife, Hak Ja Han, to be the true parents of humankind as the restored Adam and Eve.

He was a Korean religious leader best known as the founder of the Unification Church. He was born as Mun Yong-myeong on February 12, 1920. He was later known as a media mogul and an anti-communist activist. He was also well known for the Blessing Ceremony he conducted which was a mass wedding or marriage rededication ceremony, which often featured thousands of participants, usually conducted by Moon and his wife. By the time of his death, the Unification Church's organizations had become a multi-billion dollar empire.

He was born in what is now North Korea and followed their traditional Confucianist beliefs. His family became bankrupt because his older relatives devoted all the family's assets in the movement against the occupying Japanese rule. At about ten years old they converted to Christianity and joined the Presbyterian Church, where he later taught Sunday School. He graduated from a university in Tokyo with a degree in electrical engineering, in 1943.

After WWII ended and the Japanese were defeated and left Korea, in 1945, Moon began preaching his message. The beginnings of the church's official teaching, The Divine Principle, was written in 1946. It lays out the core ideology of the Unification Church and is considered by his believers to have the same status of biblical scripture. His believers are thought to be about five to seven million worldwide.

North Korean officials arrested Moon in 1946 on allegations of spying for South Korea. He was sentenced to five years in a labor camp where prisoners were routinely worked to death. He escaped 34 months later, during the Korean War, when United Nations troops advanced to the camp and the guards fled.

He and his first wife divorced in 1953. She and their son are members of the Unification Church and received the Church's Blessing. He also fathered another child with another woman in 1954. He built his first church as a refugee in Busan before formally founding Holy Spiritual Association for the Unification of World Christianity in Seoul on May 1, 1954.

Moon married his second wife, Hak Ja Han, in 1960 when she was 17, in a ceremony called the Holy Marriage. She was then called the 'True Mother' by their followers. Together they were called by the church as the True Family and their children as the True Children. In 1961 he established the Unification Church wedding or marriage rededication ceremony, known as the 'Blessing.' It is given to married or engaged couples. The first Blessing ceremony was held for 36 couples in Seoul, South Korea, all members of the church. In that ceremony, Moon matched all the couples except 12 who were already married to each other before joining the church.

In the 1960s Moon began making speeches to

audiences in the United States, Japan, and South Korea, especially talking about North Korea's aggression in Seoul, and a speech at another event in Washington, D.C. At that time he was the best known Korean in the world.

He moved to the United States in 1971, although he remained a citizen of Korea and kept a residence in South Korea. His first large conference was one sponsored by his 'International Conference on the Unity of Sciences' in Seoul in 1982 that drew 808 participants. He had previously sponsored one of the largest peaceful gatherings in history, with 1.2 million people in Yoido, South Korea. That same year he also sponsored a rally that brought 300,000 to the Washington Monument in Washington D.C.

Beginning in the 1980s, Moon and the Unification Church was influential worldwide. He met with many world leaders, endowed charitable foundations, and received accolades from every venue.

In 1982, Moon was convicted in the United States of filing false federal income tax returns and conspiracy. He served 13 months of an 18 month sentence at the Federal Correctional Institution in Danbury before being released on good behavior to a halfway house.

In September, 2005, at age 85, Moon inaugurated the Universal Peace Federation with a 120-city speaking tour. At each city, he delivered his speech titled, "God's Ideal Family - the Model for World Peace." Moon was admitted to a hospital after suffering from pneumonia, on August 14, 2012. After later suffering from organ failure, he died on September 3, 2012, at the age of 92.

Georges Ernest Roux
(1903-1981)

The Universal Alliance (French: Alliance Universelle), formerly known as Universal Christian Church (Église chrétienne universelle) and followers as Christ's Witnesses (Témoins du Christ), is a Christian-oriented new religious movement founded in France in 1952 by Georges Ernest Roux, a former postman. Roux claimed to be the reincarnation of Christ and was thus named the "Christ of Montfavet", a village on the commune of Avignon where he lived. He claimed to be Jesus, then God. He presented himself as a persecuted prophet to carry out the law of love unfulfilled by God's representatives, including Jesus.

He wrote three books containing the doctrines of the religious group, including the rejection of several dogmas commonly accepted by the main churches (Jesus' divinity and resurrection, Devil's existence and accuracy of the Gospels, among other things). Vegetarian diet, a high degree of proselytism and miraculous healings were the main practices of the organization. The group grew quickly in France and some other countries, counting several thousands of faithful, but memberships are currently on the decline.

After Roux's death in 1981, the Universal Christian Church was replaced by the Universal Alliance, a cultural association founded in August 1983 and led by one of Roux's daughters. In the 1950s, the religious group was the subject of criticisms in the media when some faithful and their children died after having refused medical treatments, and was classified as a cult in the 1995 parliamentary report established by the Parliamentary Commission on Cults in France.

Mirza Ghulam Ahmad
(Qadian, India 1835-1908)

He claimed to be the long-awaited Mahdi as well as the Second Coming and likeness of Jesus the promised Messiah at the end of time. He is the only one in Islamic history who claimed to be both. He claimed to be Jesus in the metaphorical sense; in character. He founded the Ahmadiyya Movement in 1889, envisioning it to be the rejuvenation of Islam, and claimed to be commissioned by God for the reformation of mankind.

He remains controversial by orthodox Muslims and is considered heretical because he claimed to be a non law-bearing prophet, a deputy, after Muhammad. Muslims traditionally believe Muhammad is the final prophet sent to guide mankind.

He claimed that Jesus (Isa, in Islam) had survived crucifixion and later died a natural death after having migrated toward Kasmir. He added that the notion of his physical return was therefore erroneous. He said that he had appeared in the spirit and power of Jesus. He traveled extensively across India preaching his religious ideas and won large followings within his lifetime. He is also known to have engaged in numerous debates and dialogues with Muslim, Christian, and Hindu leaders.

He also founded the Ahmadiyya Movement in Islam in 1889 whose mission, according to him, was the propagation of Islam in its pristine form. He advocated a peaceful propagation of Islam and emphatically argued against the necessity of Jihad in its military form, in the present age.

Ahmad proclaimed that he was the Promised Messiah and Mahdi and that he was fulfilment of various prophecies. This sparked great controversy, especially among the Muslim and Christian clergy. His followers say he never claimed to be the same physical Jesus who lived centuries earlier. He also claimed that just as Jesus had appeared 1400 years after the time of Moses, the promised Islamic Messiah, the Mahdi, must also appear in the 14th century after the appearance of Muhammad.

In one of his many books, he wrote about the fulfilment of various prophecies and how they related to him correlating his age and time. These include assertions that he was physically described in the Hadith and manifested various other signs, some of them being wider in scope, such as focusing on world events coming to certain points, certain conditions within the Muslim community, and varied social, political, economic, and physical conditions.

In one of his most voluminous works, he claimed to be the Messiah of Islam, which has been hard for Muslims to accept, since traditional Islamic thought maintains that Jesus will return in the flesh during the last age. According to Ahmed, the promised Mahdi was a symbolic reference to a spiritual leader and not a military leader in the person of Jesus Christ as is believed by many Muslims. Many Muslims turned against him and eventually issued a Fatwaw for his arrest and possibly execution. This was never carried out.

In 1908, he traveled to Lahore with his family and companions, and while there gave many lectures. At a large banquet arranged by dignitaries in his honor he spoke for two hours explaining his claims, teachings, and speaking to refute objections raised against him. He also preached reconciliation between Hindus and Muslims. He completed writing his last work, entitled 'Message of Peace,' a day before he died from excessive weakness. He was taken from Lahore where he died and was buried in Qadian.

Others claiming to be Christ, or thought to be Christ

by their followers include:

Yahweh ben Yahweh
(1935-2007)

He was born as Hulon Mitchell, Jr., and became a black nationalist and separatist who created the Nation of Yahweh in 1979 in Liberty City, Florida. His self-proclaimed name means "God, Son of God." He could have been deeming himself to be "son of God", not God, but many of his followers clearly deem him to be God incarnate. In 1992, he was convicted of conspiracy to commit murder and sentenced to 18 years in prison.

Wayne Bent
(1941 -)

He was also known as Michael Travesser of the Lord of Righteousness Church. He claims, "I am the embodiment of God. I am divinity and humanity combined. He was convicted in December, 2008 on one count of criminal sexual contact of a minor and two counts of contributing to the delinquency of a minor.

Ariffin Mohammed
(1943 -)

Mohammed is also known as Ayah Pin, the founder of the banned Sky Kingdom in Malaysia in 1975. He claims to have direct contact with the heavens and is believed by his followers to be the incarnation of Jesus, as well as Shiva, Buddha, and Muhammad.

Shoko Asahara
(1955 -)

He founded the controversial Japanese religious group Aum Shinrikyo, in 1984. He declared himself Christ, Japan's only fully enlightened master and the Lamb of God. His purported mission was to take upon himself the sins of the world. He outlined a doomsday prophecy which included a Third World War, and described a final conflict culminating in a nuclear Armageddon, from the term in the Bible.

According to his plan, humanity would end, except for the elite few who joined Aum. The group gained international notoriety in March 20, 1995, when it carried out the sarin gas attack on the Tokyo subway. He was sentenced to be executed for his actions.

Maurice Clemmons
(1972 - 2009)

Clemmons was an American felon responsible for the 2009 murder of four police officers in Washington State. He repeatedly referred to himself as Jesus, and said his wife Rozena was Eve, whom he went on to describe as the Goddess of all things holy.

Oscar Ramiro Ortega-Hernandez

(1990 -)

In November, 2011, he fired nine shots with an AK-47 rifle at the White House in Washington D.C., believing himself to be Jesus Christ sent to kill President Barack Obama whom he believed to be the antichrist.

Lia Eden

(1947 -)

Eden was born as Lia Aminuddin in Makassar, Indonesia. In 1998, she claimed that she met the angel Gabriel several times convincing her that she was Imam Mahdi or Messiah who brought the prophecy of the world security and justice before the doomsday. In another occasion, she also claimed that she was the reincarnation of Mother Mary and her son, Ahmad Mukti as the reincarnation of Jesus.

She also wrote a 232 page book, 'Perkenankan Aku Manjelaskan Sebuah Takdir,' meaning 'Let Me Explain a Destiny.' She gathered about 100 followers and spread her teaching in a religious group called Salamullah Pilgrim. The Indonesian Council of Ulema banned the sect for false Koran teaching. In 2006, she was sentenced to two years in prison for religious blasphemy. In 2009, she was again sentenced for another two years for the same charge.

Obama's Ring: The Seat of Satan

Chapter 4

SERPENTS AND DECEIVERS

In John's letter to the biblical church at Pergamos, he referred to Satan's seat twice. This was clearly in reference to the icon of the cult Aesculapius which was represented by the serpent. This is also the serpent that represents medicine, and it's a serpent that Barack Obama proudly displays on the ring he wears. The Apostle John called that serpent at Pergamos, the seat of Satan. Let's examine other references to serpents mentioned in the Bible that explain why God has such disdain for the serpent.

Numbers 21: 7-8

7 "Therefore the people came to Moses, and said, We have sinned, for we have spoken against the Lord, and against thee; pray unto the Lord, that he taketh away the serpents from us. And Moses prayed for the people.

53

8 And the Lord said unto Moses, Make thee a fiery serpent, and set it upon a pole: and it shall come to pass, that every one that is bitten, when he looketh upon it, shall live." (Perhaps this is the source of the serpent coiled around the staff that now represents the medical profession.)

Second Kings 18:3-4

Regarding the rule of Hezekiah in Jerusalem.

3 "And he did that which was right in the sight of the Lord, according to all that David his father did.

4 He removed the high places, and brake the images, and cut down the groves, and brake in pieces the brasen (brass) serpent that Moses had made; for unto those days the children of Israel did burn incense to it..."

Wisdom of Solomon 11:15

"Being deceived, they worshiped serpents, void of reason..."

Ecclesiasticus 21:2

"Flee from sin as from the face of a serpent; for if thou comest too near it, it will bite thee: the teeth thereof are as the teeth of a lion, slaying the souls of men."

(Remember Revelation 2, Verse 2, where John mentioned the mouth of the lion? "And the beast which I saw was like unto a leopard, and his feet were as the feet of a bear, and his mouth as the mouth of a lion: and the dragon gave him his power, and his seat, and great authority.")

Here John equates the power of the serpent with the power of the lion. Perhaps that serpent also has a great power of persuasion, as the lion roars with a great voice. John writes to stay away from it - don't listen.

Matthew 23:31-33

31 "Wherefore ye be witnesses unto yourselves, that ye are the children of them which killed the prophets.

32 Fill ye up then the measure of your fathers.

33 Ye serpents, ye generation of vipers, how can ye escape the damnation of hell?"

First Corinthians 10:6-9

6 "Now these things were our examples, to the intent we should not lust after evil things, as they also lusted.

7 Neither be ye idolators, as were some of them; as it is written. The people sat down to eat and drink, and rose up to play.

8 Neither let us commit fornication, as some of them committed, and fell in one day three and twenty thousand.

9 Neither let us tempt Christ, as some of them also tempted, and were destroyed of serpents."

Second Corinthians 11:3-4

3 "But I fear, lest by any means, as the serpent

beguiled Eve through his subtilty, so your minds should be corrupted from the simplicity that is in Christ.

4 For if he that cometh preacheth another Jesus whom we have not preached, or if ye receive another spirit, which ye have not received, or another gospel, which ye have not accepted, ye might well bear with him."

Revelation 12: 7-9

7 "And there was war in heaven: Michael and his angels fought against the dragon; and the dragon fought with his angels,

8 And prevailed not; neither was their place found any more in heaven.

9 And the great dragon was cast out, that old serpent, called the Devil and Satan, which deceiveth the whole world: he was cast out into the earth, and his angels were cast out with him."

Revelation 20:2

2 "And he laid hold on the dragon, that old serpent, which is the Devil, and Satan, and bound him a thousand years."

This list of identifiers and information about the serpent is enough to exemplify its meaning and designation. First, the emphasis of the word serpent is to designate anyone who tries to persuade a Christian to turn from God and Christianity. It's the devil in the form of a serpent in the Garden of Eden who coaxed Eve from adhering to what God told her.

How did the serpent do this? The answer is as clear to this question as the answer to the question of how are so many being led away from God and Christianity, even today. It's because those doing the coaxing are subtle and cleaver. This is what that reference in Genesis said:

> "Now the serpent was more subtil than any beast of the field which the Lord God had made."

Simply, those who lead others away from Christianity and Righteousness, and what is conscious humanity, know exactly what they are doing. They are performing the service of Satan. Satan is always trying to have his way and will use all the subtlety necessary to accomplish his mission - to fulfill evil.

One who looks in retrospect at the consequences of those deceivers shown in the last chapter would ask, "How is it possible that a person would blindly follow someone to their death, or to perform acts that are totally reprehensible to humankind?" Likely, the answer to that question is because many people lack a firm dedication to adherence to Christ's principles, and to the common expectations of humanity. They leave just enough room in their fundamental faith for Satan to slip in with his subtlety.

Isn't it almost incomprehensible to believe that common people with common human idealism could kill hundreds, thousands, and even millions of their fellow human beings? Yet, it's happened many times throughout history and it continues to happen even today. It's not unusual - it's a common event - and it should not be a great surprise if and when it happens again.

Adolph Hitler led his thousands of followers to invade and kill citizens of neighboring countries in Europe. He also led his elite corp to murder millions of Jews and other people including some severely handicapped considered 'unsuitable.' What was in the minds of those who pulled the triggers to send bullet after bullet through the heads of innocent people who merely wanted to exist, to be a threat to no one. Today, we read those facts of history and ask, "How could they allow that to happen?" Yet, if history is any indicator we will one day ask, "How did WE let that happen?" His goal that those who were convinced by 'subtlety' was to have a master race of Germans.

Joseph Stalin led inhuman atrocities against his own people in the Soviet Union. The culture of the Soviets at that time, beginning with Vladimir Lenin, was to rid the nation of the cause of its problems, the economic and social elite, except themselves. Accordingly, everyone except the proletariat, the working class, was subjected to exile or murder. Only the simple working class was spared, so long as they did exactly what they were told. By guile and subtlety the proletariat was convinced they were the chosen ones to create a new and better society.

Pol Pot is often forgotten, but he definitely shouldn't be. He also slaughtered many innocents.

When Pol Pot's Khmer Rouge gained enough power in Cambodia, in 1975, they evacuated citizens from the cities to the countryside where they were forced into communal farms. Property became communalized, and education was done at communal schools. Pol Pot's regime was extremely harsh on political dissent and opposition. Thousands of politicians and bureaucrats were killed, and Phnom Penh became a ghost town with many dying of starvation, illnesses, or execution. Land mines, Pol Pot's favorites, his 'perfect soldiers' were widely distributed around the countryside to assist other executions in the 'killing fields of Cambodia.'

The casualty list from Pol Pot's consolidation of power is disputed, but nevertheless, is a large number. One source cites three million deaths between 1975 and 1979. Another estimates 2.3 million. The Yale Genocide Projects estimates 1.7 million and Amnesty International estimated 1.4 million. Our Department of State estimated 1.2 million. Regardless which estimate is right, that's still a large number of people slaughtered by one guided by Satan.

Certainly these men were not antichrists in the truest sense because they never claimed to be Jesus, or God; and no one ever followed them under the impression they were led under the banner of God. However, their followers must have been enticed or led by the guile or subtlety of Satan to perform those vicious acts so alien to humanity. But, what about today? We would recognize Satan at work if we saw it, wouldn't we?

What guides Islamic terrorists? What guides Islamic ideology of beheading those unbelievers? What religion claims to be the followers of God, yet uses that religion to kill, maim and subjugate family members? Has Satan found an anxious and willing tool to carry out his heinous scheme to establish his power and sit on the throne in Jerusalem in the form of the antichrist - the last one - that beast? The Bible says in the last days many will be beheaded because they will not worship the beast.

And, perhaps he has a willing helper in the form of our president of the United States, Barack Hussein Obama. Obama has done more to damage the principles and concepts of Christianity in the United States than any person in the history of the United States. He blasphemes our God, the foundation of our great country, while he supports and promotes their Islamic God they call Allah. Yet when pressured for an answer, he claims to be a Christian. His actions and words now perilously mimic those described of the antichrist. He is a deceiver, perhaps a great deceiver. The source of his deception has already been disclosed. Does he wear that ring, boastfully, to demonstrate that deceptive allegiance?

Which religion does he most respect? Perhaps that's revealed in his intentions, not in his prepared text which he usually reads from a teleprompter to avoid miscalculated statements. Off text, when speaking of the Koran, he says, "The Holy Koran." When referencing the Bible, he says, "The Bible." Why does he consider the Koran holy and the Bible not holy? Is this not blasphemy? Is this not a minor slip of his deceit?

On June 28, 2006, during his 'Call to Renewal' speech, he mocked three sections of the Bible, including the Sermon on the Mount, which he called 'so radical.' He asked, mockingly, "Can either of these be used to guide public policy?" Here is that unedited part of the speech:

"Whatever we once were, we are no longer a Christian nation - not just; we are also a Jewish nation, a Muslim nation, a Buddhist nation, a Hindu nation, and a nation of nonbelievers. And even if we did have only Christians in our midst, if we expelled every non-Christian from the United States of America, whose Christianity would we teach in the schools? Would we go with James Dobson's, or Al Sharpton's? Which passages of Scripture should guide our public policy? Should we go with Leviticus, which suggests slavery is ok and that eating shellfish is abomination? How about Deuteronomy, which suggests stoning your child if he strays from the faith? Or should we just stick to the Sermon on the Mount, a passage that is so radical that it's doubtful that our own Defense Department would survive its application? So before we get carried away, let's read our bibles. Folks haven't been reading their Bibles."

This speech is certainly one of the situations that would suggest it was made from one who pretends to be of God who is not. It is deception at the highest level. He implies he has been reading the Bible while others have not. Yet, he uses out-of-context quotations to make his deceptive point.

Obama also uses his voice to turn mankind against mankind with his verbal war on successful people. He doesn't encourage those less fortunate to strive for themselves. Instead, he blames their failure on others' success and gives the assumption that he will be the great leader who will save them, perhaps bringing them all the way to the promised land. Perhaps there's a reference somewhere in the Bible about, "The Lord helps those who help themselves." If they turned their minds toward goodness and effort and their fingers from those they blame they might find that success the Lord promised - without waiting for Barack Obama to lead them to the promised land.

Barack Obama seems to want more dedicated followers with their minds focused on him and their efforts on giving him more influence and power. He has destroyed the essence, the foundation that makes America strong by these promises and actions that divide Americans. He has divided this land for his gain, his gain in more power. But, for what purpose does he turn American against American? Is it to lead them to another God or to eventually look toward him as their god? Was this one of the warnings given to Daniel?

Daniel 11: 38,39, "But in his estate shall he honour the God of forces; and a god whom his fathers knew not shall he honour with gold, and silver, and with precious stones, and pleasant things. This shall he do in the most strong holds with a strange god, whom he shall acknowledge and increase with glory; and he shall cause them to rule over many, and shall divide the land for gain."

If this is the case, if Barack Obama is using promises and actions of those pleasant things to increase another strange god or himself with glory, who is that strange god to whom he offers those things? It can only be one other, and that's the one he calls Allah, the god of Islam. He can run and hide from this concept all he wants, but many American citizens have already looked behind his facade of claiming to be a Christian. They know. He is 'dividing the land for gain' to gather enough followers to make that transition, either to that other god, or to himself as that 'strange god.'

When the numbers are large enough he will transition the United States from what was a 'Christian' nation into a Muslim nation or that godless nation of the strange god. At the moment, he has proclaimed that we are neither, but only a mixture of many. He has pushed the influence of Christianity out the back door. Or perhaps he considers growing more worthy of occupying that high place himself without another god above him.

But, as the 'deceiver,' he makes his real intentions difficult to detect. The only thing that seems certain is his goal to weaken America by dividing it. He hides his real plan by aiming his actions in such a manner that it involves two targets, thereby confusing the one that's his real intention.

On one hand he focuses his attention on actions that suggest he's leading us on the path toward socialism, and when that path becomes too visible, he shifts to another, such as the evil rich people. Is this quick hand-shuffle game of his to hide the idea that he might be a Muslim zealot in sheep's clothing? What are his real plans? Do his plans to bankrupt America fit into his scheme?

Obama's Ring: The Seat of Satan

Chapter 5

THE BEAST

Earlier in this book, I mentioned that the names Antichrist and Beast were somewhat confusing. Some believe the two are one and the same. That's possible. Perhaps those words were used interchangeably in most of the Bible, but not necessarily. The irony is that most references made about the antichrist are to the Book of Revelation, speaking of the beast and 666 concepts. In fact, the word or the description as the antichrist does not appear in Revelation. The word beast appears many times.

Perhaps some of the confusion is created from First John 2:18, which states, "Little children, it is the last time; and as ye have heard that Antichrist shall come, even now are there many Antichrists; whereby we know that it is the last time." Why is this reference confusing, and why does it seem to mean the last antichrist which will be the beast?

The concept of 'beast' and 'antichrist' could be separate and different except for one critical criteria. The antichrists claim to be Jesus, or they allow themselves to be considered God or Jesus. This special one, the beast, also allows himself to be considered Jesus, the Messiah, and eventually sits in the place of God in Jerusalem. In conclusion, although the beast has more worldly power and influence, it's still not inappropriate to consider him an antichrist, or the antichrist, the last one. When will the beast appear? It seems the old dragon will make that determination. Satan will choose the beast when he thinks the time is right. This is indicated by Revelation 13:1-2:

> "And I stood upon the sand of the sea, and saw a beast rise up out of the sea, having seven heads and ten horns, and upon his horns ten crowns, and upon his heads the name of blasphemy.
>
> 2 And the beast which I saw was like unto a leopard, and his feet were as the feet of a bear, and his mouth as the mouth of a lion: and the dragon gave him his power, and his seat, and great authority."

It's important to add another reference here to show the complete picture of when the last antichrist, the beast, will rise. This is shown in Revelation 12: 7-9:

> 7 "And there was war in heaven: Michael and his angels fought against the dragon; and the dragon fought with his angels,
>
> 8 And prevailed not; neither was their place found any more in heaven.
>
> 9 And the great dragon was cast out, that old serpent, called the Devil and Satan, which

deceiveth the whole world: he was cast out into the earth, and his angels were cast out with him."

The first verse in Chapter 13 says, "---saw a beast rise up out of the sea, having seven heads." The two operative words here are 'beast' and 'seven.' Let's consider these two words separately. First, the beast.

Consider it beast or antichrist, the last one, this is the one in Revelation. It's the same one associated with the Apocalypse, the end days. So, this one must be the real beast we've heard about regarding his mark of '666' and all the other horrendous atrocities he brings upon the earth.

Seven is considered 'God's' number. Many things, He numbered seven, including the days of the week. And, we can't forget the seven biblical churches, the seven vials of disaster, and the seven angels. Many things in the Bible and in nature have the number seven attached to them. The one most important to the identification of the beast, however, is the number seven - of the seven continents. Is there anything other than the seven continents that rise up from the sea? This critical clue is that the beast will rise when the seven heads, the seven continents are united.

Verse 2 says that's when "the dragon gave him his power, and his seat, and great authority." Since this verse includes the seven continents and 'great authority' that can only mean one thing. The beast, the last antichrist will be created when the world is under one leader. This is currently defined as 'The New World Order.' Another clue that supports this one-world concept is in Daniel 7:23, which says:

"The fourth beast shall be the fourth kingdom upon earth, which shall be diverse from all kingdoms, and shall devour the whole earth, and shall tread it down, and break it to pieces."

In this verse, Daniel refers to the 'fourth' beast which is also considered as the last beast, or the last antichrist. But, the really important part of this reference is that the fourth kingdom 'will be diverse from all kingdoms, and shall devour the whole earth.' Prior to this, all the kingdoms have included only bits and pieces of the earth, usually contained only within continents. Again, this reference says, "shall devour the whole earth, and shall tread it down, and break it to pieces." Certainly, the whole world would be a kingdom diverse from all other kingdoms.

Combining these references, it's a logical conclusion to suggest only one thing. There will come an antichrist, or beast; and he will arise when the seven continents, the whole earth is controlled by one kingdom - the one diverse from all others. Revelation 12:9, above also says Satan will deceive the 'whole world' when he was cast out of Heaven. But, what will the beast look like? How will we recognize him? To do that, let's consider the other part of Chapter 13:2:

"And the beast which I saw was like unto a leopard, and his feet were as the feet of a bear, and his mouth as the mouth of a lion–"

Why does Verse 2 continue for the purpose of describing these traits of the antichrist? To explain that he would have great authority - certainly he would influence more than just one or two countries that would attack Israel. Let's examine each trait; the leopard, the bear, and the lion, with more definition of each trait.

What's the greatest trait for which a leopard is known? A leopard is a cat. All cats are known for their

68

stealthiness, prowess, and guile. Cats ordinarily hide from their prey then sneak close enough to make a final and quick ambush. Simply, leopards are animals that sneak up on their targets. Their prey never know they are being approached until they are in the grips of the leopard.

Those who follow the antichrist will be led to follow him without realizing their great evil. The antichrist, the beast, is also referenced many times in the Bible as the deceiver. Deceit is often accomplished through subtlety. Perhaps that old dragon, the serpent, joins the leopard for this sneaky approach to ensnare his many followers.

A bear is known for its great strength. A bear does not need to be stealthy or sneaky. It merely overpowers its adversary or its prey with brute force. The antichrist will have a strong nature that will inspire others to follow his strength and strong persuasion. His strong leadership over those ten strong countries that follow him is again mentioned in Daniel 7:20:

> "And of the ten horns that were in his head, and of the other which came up, and before whom three fell; even of that horn that had eyes, and a mouth that spake very great things, whose look was more stout than his fellows."

The word 'stout' as with the strength of a bear might be interpreted in many ways. The free online dictionary gives several definitions:

1. Having or marked by boldness, bravery or determination; firm and resolute.
2. Strong in body; sturdy.

3. Strong in structure or substance; solid or substantial.

4. Bulky in figure; thickset or corpulent.

5. Powerful; forceful.

6. Stubborn or uncompromising.

It's clear from these definitions that this antichrist, this beast, will have at least one strong characteristic. He will be powerful and forceful; as A bear is powerful and forceful. He will be unyielding and uncompromising.

Other than strength and fierceness, what other trait gives a lion its common recognition? Its roar. A lion is recognized for its commanding roar, its loud noise. That beast that rose out of the sea also had 'a mouth that spake very great things.' Other sections of the Bible repeat this description by identifying the beast as a man of voice, or of having voice. This man, this beast, this antichrist, definitely is described as one who will be a great and persuasive speaker. Those who listen will hear his great voice roar. Many will be deceived and persuaded especially at the end times.

Perhaps the end times are not near, at least within the next few years. And, now that the antichrist does not exist as the appointed one. He will exist when Satan decides to give him that power. Presently, that person is building his base to become the antichrist, saying great things to deceive his followers that they should trust and worship his leadership. But, how will we recognize the end times? How will we recognize the antichrist is among us?

In Daniel 12:6, Daniel asked that question during his vision with the Lord. " - How long shall it be to the end of these wonders?"

In the next verse, the Lord answered, " - it shall be

70

for a time, times, and a half; and when he shall have accomplished to scatter the power of the holy people, all these things shall be finished."

Another clue comes from Daniel 7:23, which says, "The fourth beast shall be the fourth kingdom upon earth, which shall be diverse from all kingdoms, and shall devour the whole earth, and shall tread it down, and break it in pieces."

Two concepts are important in these short references. First, the whole earth is recognized. Obviously this would include the seven continents. Christ would certainly have known about the 'whole earth' including the other continents unknown to mankind at that time.

Also, in the end times He explains that the power of the holy people will be scattered, diminished. No one can deny this has not already happened to the United States and the world. Even Barack Obama announced that condition when he stated on June 28, 2006, "Whatever we once were, we are no longer a Christian nation, at least not just; we are also a Jewish nation, a Muslim nation, a Buddhist nation, a Hindu nation, and a nation of nonbelievers." Even Barack Obama has acknowledged that the power of the holy people has been scattered.

Another observation must be made concerning this 'Call to Renewal' speech. Watching a video of that speech created a deeper question; did he mean the United States is no longer a Christian nation. He paused, as if an afterthought, before he added that the United States includes other religions. That made the intentions of that comment very uncertain. In either case, it was a blasphemous statement regarding the power of the holy people, especially Christians. Perhaps we should consider other statements and acts of blasphemy by Barack Obama that demonstrate the power of the holy people has been scattered. Perhaps he is the one who has been at the forefront of scattering the power of the holy people. Revelation 13:5-6 reveals more of the beast's traits and characteristics:

> 5 "And there was given unto him a mouth speaking great things and blasphemies.
>
> 6 "And he opened his mouth in blasphemy against God, to blaspheme his name, and his tabernacle, and them that dwell in heaven."

These references describe two characteristics of the beast, the antichrist; oratory and blasphemy. How does Barack Obama fulfill this description?

He said he is not a Muslim, but during an interview with George Stephanopoulos on September 7, 2008, he referenced, "My Muslim faith." If he is a Muslim, why does he continue to deny it? Is he trying to be deceptive, and for what purpose? The Books of Daniel and Revelation also identify the 666 beast as the deceiver. Could Obama be fulfilling this role?

Another blatant blasphemy occurred on April 16, 2009 by the Obama group. On that date he required the monogram, consisting of the letters IHS, for the name of Jesus, be covered before he made his speech at Georgetown University. The monogram above an archway was covered with black painted plywood. Certainly he would not consider this blasphemy - black painted plywood covering the symbol of Jesus.

Obama was also recorded at a closed-door fund raiser in San Francisco making disparaging comments about religion. He said, "You go into these small towns in Pennsylvania and, like a lot of small towns in the Midwest, it's not surprising they get bitter, they cling to guns and religion or antipathy to people who aren't like them or anti-immigrant sentiment or anti-trade sentiment as a way to explain their frustrations."

His comment didn't specifically say Christians but that's the dominant religion referred to in the Midwest. A reference that clinging to religion (Christianity) out of bitterness and frustration and not out of search for truth and salvation is another bold example of his common blasphemy against Christ and the Bible.

Several places in the Bible say or suggest that many will come to worship the beast. Perhaps that worship has already started, even before the beast has been recognized and appointed by Satan. One reference, Revelation 13:8 states,

> "And all that dwell upon the earth shall worship him, whose names are not written in the book of life of the lamb slain from the foundation of the world."

One such of those worships has already been recorded with a video on Youtube. This video recorded a gathering of the Gamaliel Organization, on December 8, 2008, where some members prayed to Barack Obama, "Hear our cry, Obama," and "Deliver us, Obama."

In response to a press release by the president of the Gamaliel Foundation on October 2, 2009, which refuted that claim and said the members were praying, "Hear our cry, oh God," I listened to the video several more times. Although the audio was rather muffled and distorted, the pleas are clearly aimed at Obama, not to God. Below is the video URL. (http://www.youtube.com/watch?v=JTOZkwrxPao)

The list of Obama's anti-Christian actions, rhetoric,

and blasphemies is too long to identify each individually. A casual review of his actions and comments against churches, especially the Catholic Church, Defense of Marriage Act, cabinet appointments, and exclusion of Christian leaders from religious events are clear proof that he has no respect for God, Christian values, or any reference to the value foundation that allowed the formation of our great country - The United States of America.

But, is the antichrist working now, and how will he show himself? The antichrist will be recognized as a 'man of peace' worshiped by millions, until the restrainer is removed. Then the beast will show himself. This question of the restrainer is identified in Second Thessalonians 3:6-8:

> "And now ye know what witholdeth that he might be revealed in his time." "For the mystery of iniquity doth already work; only he who now letteth will let, until he be taken out of the way." "And then shall that Wicked be revealed - ." The New King James Version states, "For the mystery of lawlessness is already at work; only who now restrains will do so until He is taken out of the way."

Until the beast shows his real self, he will be considered a peacemaker, and even one who sits in the place of Jesus, even in the place of God by some ardent worshipers. At one time he will even sit in Jerusalem and proclaim that he is the returned Christ.

Much confusion exists pertaining to this event when the restrainer is removed. Many consider it a time when the Holy Spirit is removed from earth and everything becomes lawless. Some consider this the time of Rapture when those who worship Christ are removed from earth, leaving only the ungodly remaining in mortal form on earth until the time of the Millennium; that time being when Christ and those who did not support the 666 beast will reign on earth for the next thousand years.

Some believe either they or their friends who are Christians will suddenly disappear, and everybody will wonder where they went. This is not what the Bible explains will happen. Only their souls will be resurrected, not their bodies. They will not suddenly disappear. According to Revelation, Chapter 20, Verse 4:

"And I saw the souls of them that were beheaded for the witness of Jesus, and for the word of God, and which had not worshiped the beast, neither had received his mark upon their foreheads, or in their hands; and they lived and reigned with Christ a thousand years."

Simply, this means that those who refuse to accept the mark of the beast, or worship his name, will be killed, beheaded. Without anyone now opposing his reign of terror, the beast is free to begin his reign of terror directed by Satan. This is a warning that when that time comes, everybody will have to make the decision of whether to accept the mark of the beast, or be killed. This is a time of serious consequences. These horrendous actions will take place after the restrainer is 'taken out of the way.' Again, who is this restrainer?

While many still believe the restrainer is the Holy Spirit, this idea must be questioned. If the Holy Spirit were already 'taken out of the way' why would it be necessary for those Christian believers who refused to accept the beast's mark to be killed. The beast's evil reign would already have begun for that to happen. The Holy

Spirit would still be here in the bodies of those being killed by beheading. Perhaps we should look more at the current geopolitical situation to determine what restrainer must be removed for the beast to expose his real intent.

Although the beast's foremost goal is to sit as God in the Temple in Jerusalem, his arrogance and ego will be so great that he must also be worshiped along the way before he reaches that high place. Even to get to an intermediate step he must have the freedom to do so. He must be free to trample on the people of the world so he can be worshiped even if by brute force and evil tactics. Anyone who would be that openly evil, especially to directly attack the main prize, Israel, would have to consider what role the United States would play in protecting Israel.

Presently, the United States is the primary and most obvious obstacle to that attack. As discussed before, the restrainer couldn't be the Holy Spirit, because those possessing the Holy Spirit will be under attack until the very end. Many having the Holy Spirit within them will be beheaded by the beast's followers after he is unrestrained to show his full wrath as the antichrist. That restrainer to prevent the antichrist from venting his pure evil is the United States. The strength and influence of the United States must be destroyed before the antichrist can have his free will.

The only realistic and imaginable 'restrainer' at this time is the strength and influence of the United States. We have already said how that strength and status is being viciously attacked. Obama's administration is myopically focused on bankrupting America. A bankrupt America is an impotent and weak America, and would leave not only Israel vulnerable to attack, but the rest of the world as well. Once America falls, the world falls; it falls right into the ready grip of the deadly antichrist; appointed, guided, and promoted by that great dragon, Satan.

This calls into question another obstacle the antichrist must overcome before he has full control. That is the influence and strength of Christianity in the world, especially America. Christianity serves not only a path to personal salvation into the eternal life hereafter, it also serves as a moral compass for daily living and human relationships.

This moral compass is the unique lifeline that guided those who established this great country. It's the moral compass that's guided its prosperity and well-being. It's the moral compass that positioned America to be the great hope for humanity and the world. It's now the same moral compass that's being trampled upon and 'scattered' to no longer set a guiding path. There are many biblical examples where turning from this moral compass, turning from God, has resulted in monumental consequences.

The first example was Noah and the great flood. Of course there are those who protest that this event never happened. But, those who believe the lessons of the Bible know it did happen in one form or another. Whether the flood covered the entire earth or not, there is evidence that the flood did cover the known world at that time in what has been called the cradle of civilization. Ancient artifacts have been discovered in those areas where the water has receded in recent years to suggest life was plentiful there at one time. Then it was flooded.

According to the Bible, when mankind became so evil, God eliminated that evil from earth with the flood. Noah and his family were spared because they never gave up their faith in God.

This biblical account of that flood is not the only reference to a great flood at or near that time. Ancient Sumerian cuneiform writings on tablets describe the Epic of Gilgamesh, which records a great flood in that same area. Almost complete writings of the epic dating 2200 B.C. have been found. Fragmented tablets of the event have been found dating as far back as 3300 B.C. Sumeria along with Ur are considered by many as the oldest known established communities in the world.

The Jewish people also suffered when they turned their ways from God, from that moral compass. They were scattered to all corners of the globe until 1948, when a place was made for them in what was Palestine. Certainly guided by God, after having paid for their transgressions, they were allowed to recapture and reclaim their ancient homeland. Since 1948 the Jewish people have succeeded in keeping their land and their beliefs although attacked many times by overwhelming forces. Has it been luck, the guiding hand of God, or some other secret power that has allowed them to persevere?

This presents the question of our time. With world-wide geopolitics forming against Israel, will Israel continue to survive? Will the United States be a factor in that security and survival? A discussion on the relevance of Iran and their Mahdi, regarding this question, will be introduced later.

Another example of God's wrath against those who would deny him and turn their ways from his warnings are the fates of Sodom and Gomorrah. Although the words are not specific and graphic in that Bible story, the words are sufficient to explain that those two cities had become so fixated on sexual deviation that God wanted to rid the world of such wickedness.

According to that story, God sent two angels to warn Lot and his family, who were not part of those transgressions, to leave because the city would be destroyed. While the two angels visited, the citizens of Sodom were so sexually corrupt that upon seeing them go into Lot's home, they wanted to 'know' them. The angels knew what was happening and told Lot and his family to, "Get out of here right now, and don't look back." As they left, Lot's wife made the mistake of looking back. Again, artifacts recently discovered in that area near the Dead Sea suggest the two sites of Sodom and Gomorrah described in that Bible story. The findings also show the two cities were probably destroyed by volcanic eruptions that spewed fire and burning sulphur over them. The artifacts date from the middle bronze age, which would have been the time period Sodom and Gomorrah existed.

Another theory proposes that a large asteroid struck farther away and spewed debris high into the air, eventually much of which landed in the area of the Dead Sea, including Sodom and Gomorrah. Ice core samples of that period suggest the asteroid debris coverage could have been world-wide, even changing climatic conditions in that area.

Will God turn his eyes from the United States and destroy our strength and position, and the hope for mankind? Absolutely not. That's not the way God works. God is there always, waiting for our hands and our thoughts to reach out and touch His. He will not abandon us - we are fast abandoning Him. Satan is preparing the way for the antichrist to have his way when Satan selects him and gives him that great authority. He is steadily scattering, diminishing, the influence of Christian principles. The Obama administration is a key component of that destructive preparation.

Obama's Ring: The Seat of Satan

Chapter 6

BANKRUPTING AMERICA

While in principle I agree with Obama that the United States, as well as the world, should move to renewable energy for our long-term energy resources, nevertheless that transition should be in a more controlled and compassionate manner. His exhibited energy policy thus far has been 'full speed ahead with the transition, and American citizens be damned.'

His refusal to expand fossil fuel exploration and extraction continues to penalize the weak and the poor, and adds to our national debt every day. Obviously, he is trying to make the transition immediately, which demonstrates either his out-of-touch with reality blind charge into more bankruptcy for our nation - or that's part of his plan to destroy the nation by subterfuge. A reasonable thinking leader would demonstrate more concern and compassion for those depending on that leader for normal existence.

Is he not aware that his inactions to make the United States energy independent puts our country in danger both economically and militarily? Or is he aware of the danger, and simply does not care? Any reasonably intelligent person can easily visualize and understand that danger, especially with all the terrorist hazards developing against us throughout the world. Or, is there another possible reason that will be discussed later for his apparent intention to weaken the United States?

Reportedly, the United States has more fossil-based resources under our land than Saudi Arabia. Including shale and coal deposits we probably have more energy resources under our dirt and water than all other countries combined. Yet, we continue to import foreign oil and penalize our domestic producers when they venture forth to build America's strength. What is the man's problem with simple logic and simple arithmetic? Let's consider an example of his support for domestic energy production.

One of our president's senior environmental representatives said they will crucify the first five who try to develop more fossil fuel so America can become fuel independent and prosperous once again. Ah, to digress to world mediocrity and below. Specifically, this is what EPA representative Al Armendariz said in 2010:

"But as I said, oil and gas is an enforcement priority, it's one of seven, so we are going to spend a fair amount of time looking at oil and gas production. And I gave, I was in a meeting once and I gave an analogy to my staff about my philosophy of enforcement, and I think it was probably a little crude and maybe not appropriate for the meeting but I'll go ahead and tell you what I said. It was kind of like how the Romans used to conquer little villages in the Mediterranean. They'd go into a little

Turkish town somewhere, they'd find the first five guys they saw and they would crucify them. And then you know that town was really easy to manage for the next few years. And so you make examples out of people who are in this case not compliant with the law. Find people who are not compliant with the law, and you hit them as hard as you can and you make examples out of them, and there is a deterrent effect there. And, companies that are smart see that, they don't want to play that game, and they decide at that point that it's time to clean up. And, that won't happen unless you have somebody out there making examples of people. So you go out, you look at an industry, you find people violating the law, you go aggressively after them. And we do have some pretty effective enforcement tools. Compliance can get very high, very, very quickly. That's what these companies respond to is both their public image but also financial pressure. So you put some financial pressure on a company, you get other people in that industry to clean up very quickly. So, that's our general philosophy."

Our progressive leader has such great plans for our future. Perhaps his plans will lead us to even greater environmental progress: candles and bicycles. Who needs electricity, cars, and highways, anyway? Would it be too complicated for Obama to consider that renewable energy must be planned over a longer transition time that allows consistency and dependability without disrupting life as it exists today? That is unless his plan is to create that disruption and to create a lifestyle for all Americans comparable to that of third-world countries. He has never given a strategic plan or any timetable for an energy transition. He keeps proceeding blindly ahead without acknowledging any circumstances from that blind charge.

He also continues to pour millions of taxpayer dollars into those failing renewable energy companies. Is his plan to help create energy or to help expedite bankruptcy of our nation?

He proudly proclaims his zeal to help the middle-class and poor in our society, but is that what he really has in mind? His speeches are all about helping those who have less than the evil rich people get their fair share. Yet, his actions are directly opposed to achieving that humanitarian goal. While he proudly and boastfully talks of putting more money in their front pockets, he steals even more from their wallets and bank accounts. He robs their few precious assets from them as he convinces them he is their savior that will give them more. How does this happen?

Most people not considered wealthy must put gasoline in their automobiles to get to work. Half of what they pay for gasoline is money that Obama's policies strips from their available assets. That's money that could be used for many other things that might help stimulate the economy.

Due to his energy policy of not allowing more oil drilling in and around the United States, gasoline prices have doubled since he became president in 2008. That's doubled! When he took office, gasoline was approximately $1.85 per gallon. At this moment, it's over $3.60 per gallon. That means people are penalized as much as $100.00 to $200.00 a month for gasoline - just to get to their jobs. And those needy people still consider Barack Obama their hero and savior? Obviously, once a savior is recognized, he is never questioned by his worshipers.

His attack on American energy production has increased costs in every sector of the American economy, thereby penalizing the poor and middle-class the most. How? The answer is simple. The cost of energy determines the cost of almost everything in our modern society.

Electricity and power bills have increased for the

average consumer because the president has curtailed available energy resources. The poor and middle-class have to pay more for electricity and heat, even if heated by other than electricity. With less production of coal, that cost has also increased, or those who had used coal for heating have had to convert to other heat sources. These increased energy costs are also suffered by businesses and factories who must also increase the cost of their products and services to remain in business. The falling domino effect runs the course until the final inflated costs reach the consumer - largely the poor and middle class who are hurt the worst. But, by keeping his finger pointed at the wealthy, Obama continues to be the savior of the poor and middle-class. They close their eyes as they fold their hands in prayer to him.

And, we should not forget the effects of ethanol. Although this was an active program long before Barack Obama was elected president, he still has done nothing to curtail its devastating effects. Let's consider just a few.

First, many people report engine problems with their automobiles from using ethanol. When ethanol was first introduced it was to support two needs; less reliance on oil, since at that time the oil price was beginning to escalate faster. And, the major purpose for its introduction was to be more environmentally friendly. This was partially in response to the 'climate change' promoters who were determined to make money with their great scare tactics. (Has Al Gore ever admitted how wealthy he became with his great 'save the world' environmental program?) Many engines are having to be repaired from the damage created by ethanol use.

Again, Barack Obama puts a dagger through the economic hearts of the poor and middle-class, who often can't afford those repairs. Yet, they continue to believe his promises that his sole purpose as president is to give them their 'fair share.' Could he mean a fair share of despair, not their fair share of the country's wealth?

Cost of repairing automobile engines however is not necessarily the greatest disaster created by the use of ethanol against the poor and middle-class. Often, that's a one-time cost that can be absorbed with payments on credit cards or by giving up some other family necessity. The greatest cost to those who can afford it least is the increased cost of food. Even the least wealthy must have food, and nowadays there are not enough personal gardens to fulfill that need. Only a few people now have a garden, a cow, chickens and pigs from which they can get their food. Most people now must buy their food from the grocery store. So, how does ethanol affect the price of food?

At this time, most ethanol is made from corn. Corn is also used many other ways, especially related to other food, many foods that one would not imagine as an added ingredient for improved taste, firming a product, color, or to create different blends of another food product. Corn is also used as a livestock food. In effect, corn is used in most things related to food and food production. What happens when much of that corn product is transferred to produce ethanol? Have you noticed the price of food, lately? Are you aware that a gallon of milk has skyrocketed from $1.99 two years ago to over $4.00 today? Have you seen the price of beef, or has that price become so expensive you can no longer buy beef? Have you seen the price of any food product, and can say it has not increased in price at least 25 percent during the past two years? The price of all food has increased, and for four reasons:

First, is the normal rise in inflation. This ordinarily should be no more than 5 percent unless the economy is really booming. Our economy is barely creeping.

Second, is the increased cost to transport that food, because Obama is keeping the price of gasoline too high. It costs more to move that corn to factories and to move those products from factories to the distributors then to the store shelves.

Third, is increased costs of retailers for wages and salaries of workers to meet their increased costs for their gas to get to work, and their cost for higher priced food. Now they will have an added cost to cover the increased health care demands under the new health care law. When that new requirement gets into full bloom, is there any imagination that food prices will not skyrocket even higher?

Fourth, is corn availability, depending upon the financial market and weather. Prices are kept as high as possible by market controllers, and peak prices are compounded even more when a drought, or the threat of a drought occurs. Even at this moment, a drought is forecast for the next corn-growing season. Even during a drought Obama will not be deterred from throwing more money at the basic problem, by corn producer subsidies to keep them in business, so the price of food can remain high.

If the price for a gallon of milk rises to $6.00 a gallon next year, what effect will that have on everyone, especially children who need milk to help develop their bones and teeth? What if the price of all food continues to rise? Will Obama blame those increased costs on normal inflation and price gougers in the marketplace? He certainly will blame it on someone else as he always does, although he is now encouraging the ethanol level to be raised to 15 percent - again devastating the buying power of those who support him most, and even worship him.

Never would he look into a mirror and say, "That's

the man who deprives the poor and middle-class from their 'fair share' by raising prices so high that what money they have will buy less of their bare necessities." In effect, Obama's actions regarding his energy policy, or lack thereof, takes money from the pockets of those who need it most.

For wealthy people, Obama's energy policy is merely an inconvenience. For the non-wealthy it's a critical burden that restricts their health, their future, and their happiness. Yet, those loyal followers to whom he has made those empty promises believe his every word as if spoken from God. They will continue to keep their eyes closed as he destroys their future, condemns them to poverty, and rips apart the foundation of the United States of America.

Although Obama is their savior, he continues to destroy their well-being by his secrets and deceptions. His followers are blindly oblivious to the fact that his war on wealthy people is a war on all people. His blind followers will continue to suffer most. He must maintain this rift between economic classes to continue his total takeover of America.

Currently, Obama has not established a dollar figure that defines the wealthy. Is it $200,000 or is it a million dollars? Most certainly it will be an amount that he can easily change as he gains more power and can become more dictatorial.

Health Care

Another deception by Barack Hussein Obama was the implementation of his so-called Affordable Care Act. While campaigning for this program he promised many things to many people to have his name attached to a signature program that once enacted will carry his name forever. Many things he promised simply were untruths.

He promised that if you liked your current doctor, you could keep that same doctor. In many cases this statement was false because insurance programs were changed that shifted doctors to different programs. Other doctors had to change the status of their practices that moved them to different locations. Due to certain restrictions they couldn't operate within the same cost limitations. Consequently, in many cases this promise was false; you can't keep your same doctor.

He also said taxes would not be raised to fund the new health care program. Instead of identifying the increased cost of the program he tried to catagorize the increased costs as mandates, not taxes. He failed to disclose that many more taxes would be placed on health care support services such as prosthetics providers and other equipment manufacturers. As his health care program becomes more fully disclosed many more taxes, restrictions, and mandates expose themselves that increase the tax burden on everyone.

In effect, the health care law he enacted was not only presented based on falsehoods, and as presented to the Supreme Court was unconstitutional. The Chief Justice of the Supreme Court rewrote the law by changing the word 'mandates' to the word 'taxes.' Although the semantics are different the results are the same. The government will get more money from more people leaving less money for citizens, especially poor citizens, to buy food and other basic necessities.

During the court challenge process, those costs were determined to be taxes. Again, the man was brazen enough to think people should believe his deceptions. The tragedy is that too many people do. They agree with anything he says, even if they are staring the lie right in the eye as he says it. They are dedicated and loyal followers of this Pied Piper of deceit. To them, he can do no wrong or ill will toward the United States or its citizens.

Obama also stated another falsehood to support his health care plan. He said that 716 billion dollars was not taken out of Medicare to help fund the new health care program. He said only that amount of waste was taken out of Medicare. Two observations must be made in that regard.

First, if there were Medicare waste or fraud, why wasn't that amount taken from Medicare before the new health care law was enacted? Did he and his administration feel Medicare waste was appropriate until they needed that money for another purpose?

Second, I was personally affected by the removal of those funds from Medicare. On a recent visit to my eye doctor, optometrist, I was charged an extra $33.00 for that normal eye examination. I had never been charged extra for an eye exam before. The doctor said Medicare no longer covered that part of the examination. During that same week I also visited my dermatologist for a skin problem. My regular doctor had been replaced by a physician's assistant. Does Obama consider a regular doctor as waste in Medicare?

Budget Deficit and Debt

When Barack Obama was campaigning for office of the presidency before the 2008 election the national debt was four trillion dollars. He claimed it was unpatriotic for then President George Bush to allow the national debt to get that high. He promised he would reduce the national debt if he were elected president. It's four times greater than when he took office.

Today, as I write this book the national debt is sixteen trillion dollars - and rising. Barack Obama has quadrupled the national debt in only four years. According to his own words, he must be four times as unpatriotic as

George Bush. Perhaps his dislike for America is even greater than that. When will he consider spending restraints within America's ability to pay? Or, does he even care what happens when America runs out of money to pay for anything?

His vicious attack on 'rich people' is only a ruse to keep Americans separated, so they don't focus on a single bonding ideology. If Americans became united as one country aiming at one goal - continued progress for everyone - Obama would lose his strength base to progress toward his ultimate goal. His disregard for long-term financial consequences for America seems aimed at only his personal power ambitions. That will be discussed later.

As stated earlier, he must keep American citizens divided. He does this by suggesting that unless rich people pay more into the government, so he can give more of that richness to the underprivileged, they are being cheated by those rich people. Without considering the consequences of what he says, they believe him.

What they don't understand, and don't question, is that given the increased taxes he proposes for rich people, the change in the budget deficit or the national debt would not even be noticeable. No more could be given to the poor, no more could be bought to improve our country, and the national debt would not be decreased. Obama is simply giving his supporters and worshipers a false illusion.

Compared to what Obama spends, that extra tax on the wealthy affects absolutely no one, other than the wealthy being taxed. In reality, those who need jobs and more income will be more negatively affected. The wealthy will have less money to help create more jobs those less wealthy need. Even those who have adequate funds to create new jobs will be reluctant to do so. They are uncertain how much more Obama plans to take from them in the future. This is another of Obama's proposals that will continue his rush to bankrupt a nation - our nation.

Summary

Obama's open and blatant determination to get more rich people to pay their fair share is a ruse beyond comprehension. His statement is that the money is needed to cover the deficit and pay down the debt. For those who are confused by this difference, the national debt is the amount the United States owes other countries and bond holders for loans to keep the government running. The budget deficit is the amount needed in the current fiscal year to pay for obligations committed for that one year's activity. Although he claims the money is needed for either of those requirements that is not what will happen to any additional taxes gained from taxing rich people more.

If his normal trend continues, any additional revenue gained from more taxes from rich people will be spent before it gets into the treasury to cover the deficit or the debt. Obama has an insatiable urge to spend more, whether funds are available for those expenditures or not. The classic example is the money he plans to spend from that saved by winding down the wars in Iraq and Afghanistan.

He claims that money can be used elsewhere, when in fact that money does not exist. It will be new borrowed money that will undoubtedly put us deeper in debt with China. Yet, his words drip like honey as a promise to his unquestioning worshipers that he will give more of that available money to them. That's his promise that they will have more free Obamaphones and all the accessories that come with those free Obamaphones.

As discussed before, the amount scheduled to be confiscated from rich people will not be enough to make a small dent in either the deficit or the national debt. Its impact will be minuscule and totally irrelevant. Which presents the new question - what will Obama do when the inconsequential impact that little money will have becomes obvious? How will he explain that great shortfall to his followers?

He will have only two choices. First, he can borrow more money from China, if Congress agrees to raise the debt ceiling. Or second, he can adjust the classification of the level of rich people. Now, it's uncertain at what level of income he classifies as rich people. That number seems somewhere between $250,000 a year and a million dollars. Perhaps after the first step has been approved, he will suddenly determine that people making over $50,000 a year are rich. Each of these options has dire considerations.

Understanding the dire fiscal situation America now faces, something drastic must happen to even present the facade that our government is trying to do what's right. Obama has the open forum to make the case that Congress must increase the debt ceiling, or seniors will starve, and children will be without clothes and thrown out in the street to starve and freeze. He has the forum and the 'great voice' to convince his followers of that condition. Consequently, Congress has no choice but to raise the debt ceiling when he makes his request. What will be the limit to the amount of debt he plans for the United States - and why? Has he no limit? Any reasonable person understands limits.

Let's assume your annual income is $50,000, and after taxes you have $45,000 net income. That allows expenditures of approximately $3700 a month. After fixed costs such as house payments, car payments, insurance for the house and car, and other payments that are unavoidable, you have $1700 to spend for other things such as food, electricity, gasoline, clothing, home repairs, automobile repairs, school supplies for your children, doctor bills, dental bills, recreation, cell phones, the internet, and television. You barely make enough to keep your head above water at the end of each month.

Then suddenly you have unexpected additional expenses. Your automobile has a major breakdown and you have to add a thousand dollars to your credit card to keep it running so you can get to your job. Another crisis occurs when your son loses his job and moves back in while he searches for another job, but the jobs that he like are not available. That's another mouth to feed, more clothes to buy, more gasoline to put in your son's car so he can look for a job.

The economy gets so bad that your working hours are reduced and your income is now ten percent less than it was. You start adding another thousand dollars each month onto your credit card, hoping you can pay off the credit card when the economy improves. Then you fall behind with your credit card payment and the interest rate is raised from ten percent to sixteen percent. Suddenly the interest on the credit card loan is so great that all you can pay is just the interest.

You get the picture facing many American citizens today. Many must make a serious choice between reducing the things they want, or declaring bankruptcy and starting over. On the other hand, perhaps there is another choice.

Instead of continuing to spend, why not reduce those nonessentials until the credit card is paid off, or the economy improves and the job hours increase; and that son who's waiting for his special job gets a job to help the family survive. If necessary, a family can survive without television and the internet awhile. The family vacation trip can wait two more years without undue hardship. Not everyone in the family needs a cell phone. Once adjusted, sometimes the simple life is a great life. That's the way I grew up; without electricity, a phone, television, and especially not a vacation trip. My greatest dream as a youth was to get a job, any job. I survived - and now I'm probably the happiest person in the whole wide world. I understand what success is when you work for it and achieve it. Success is not having more things; it's knowing your diligent and dedicated efforts have rewarded you with things you deserve.

This scenario of an individual family's financial condition is an example of what happened when our economy was weakened starting with the housing market collapse. The economy took a dive which is similar to a family with lost or declining income. When the economy slows, less taxes are coming into the national treasury. As with a family, when less money comes in a choice must be made to cut expenses, or to get a second job to pay for the things wanted, not necessarily for all the things needed.

The government can't take a second job. Therefore, to keep from reducing costs, the government considers taking more taxes from its citizens as that second job. The great difference is that the government does not make the same effort and sacrifice as one who must work more. They simply take it without earning it. To reduce spending is government's least desired option, at least for a government that enjoys spending. Recently, Obama even said, "Our national debt is not a problem, and will not be for at least another ten years," although our national debt is now about 16 trillion dollars.

Our government is spending too much on things we want, not necessarily what we need. Obama wants to keep enlarging the credit card limit so he can keep spending to win more followers and worshipers. He must buy their love and loyalty to insure he has the power position for his future plans.

To him it doesn't matter if that unlimited credit goes well beyond the ability to pay. That will be America's problem when he leaves office - if he leaves office. In either case, if he keeps spending on things his followers want, he will have a following that will give him unlimited power. That power could be used to transform America, as he promised, or it could be used to affect new world changes. What are his plans? Why does he intend to bankrupt the United States of America? His plan is not an accident, and it's not from incompetence. It's a deliberate plan to bankrupt America. Many of these answers are exposed in the next chapters.

Chapter 7

OUR FUTURE

It's inconceivable that Barack Obama could or would give up the powerful position of the presidency of the United States at the end of his current term. His demeanor has always been too stern, arrogant, and uncompromising, or as that reference in the Bible says in Daniel 7:20; more 'stout.' It's always been his way, or no way. The man clearly has a power lust that will not be satisfied with the feeling of a job-well-done at the end of this term. He will not go into the background gracefully as did his predecessor, George Bush; the man he used as a whipping post to demonize so harshly.

In the spirit of a true gentleman, a proud American, and a loving Christian, George Bush has never lashed back to criticize Barack Obama, or any of his policies. Barack Obama does not demonstrate that character. So, what does that mean for the future of America?

Obama is too young to go quietly into the background and play the role of the grand old man of politics. He can't do that. He has been and will continue to be driven by his uncontrolled power lust: the leopard, bear, and lion. He is destiny-driven. And, from my vision as a fiction writer and from my research, especially from the Bible, I can see only one or two courses he is likely to take. One is a major disaster for a democratic and free United States, the other a major disaster for the world. Depending on the order, it could be both.

Let's consider the first possibility, with the understanding that I'm a fiction writer. After all, I really am. I've already written six novels. Two of those novels consider the same situation of which I am about to explain fictionally here. This first scenario (fictionally of course) is that he will assume power and control over the United States at the end of his elected term. I almost wrote 'duly elected term' but there's some question about the propriety of the past election process; therefore, I will just say his current elected term.

In my book, 'America 20XX: The New World Order,' I used the president's name as President Arabar. For simplicity I will use that name here. Of course, the other names in this short scenario will also be fictitious, but will serve the common purpose.

FUNDAMENTAL CHANGE

President Arabar knew he had nothing to lose at the beginning of his second term in office as president of the United States. He knew the only thing he had to be careful of was not to allow enough information to be revealed about himself that he could be impeached and removed from office. However, he also knew even if that were to happen, it wouldn't cause a major problem for the outcome of his destiny.

The rest of the world loved him and worshiped him, and would continue to do so, regardless. He knew those who worshiped him would feel he was crucified because of his race if he were impeached, and would worship him even more. If Congress challenged him, he knew he could bury them in shame and disgrace. His reverie, looking out the large window, was disturbed by his chief of staff, William Curtain, as he opened the door and walked in.

"Mister President," he said, "your select staff has arrived. Shall I ask them to come in?"

"Of course, we need to get started."

Each graciously shook the president's hand before they took their designated seats around the large oval table. The president's senior advisor, Melanie Harrett, sat to his right, and his secretary of defense, Henry Carlton, sat to his left. Other members of his select staff included the secretary of homeland security, Jeanette Grapalo, and heads of the two major security agencies, the CIA and the FBI. His attorney general, Alex Hand was also there.

The president waited for the others to get comfortable in their seats before he began. "As you know, we came a long way during my first administration. We divided the United States enough to maintain almost total control in the future as far as we can see." He turned to Harrett and added, "We can all thank my senior advisor for most of that accomplishment. She was most instrumental in selecting the cabinet members and other advisors to support our cause."

"Thank you for your trust and confidence in me, Mr. President. But, after we planned for so long to undertake this program, it wasn't difficult to find others who had plans already in place to fundamentally change America. They were eagerly panting on the sidelines."

"Nevertheless, you chose those ready to go when I was first elected."

The chief of staff, Curtain, added, "That was a clever plan. While you, Mister Persident, distracted your critics and America with the big hammer, the others sliced bits and pieces off America's strength with perfect precision. The cabinet heads and other appointed czars did their appointed tasks perfectly with their subtle and devious policies and regulations."

Harrett again thanked those praising her work in designating perfect personnel for the jobs they were assigned. She said she had two great disappointments during that time. These were the assignments of Carnita Dunnigan and Vic Hones. "It's too bad their communist ideologies were discovered before they could have accomplished more of their assignments. We could have accomplished so much more if they had stayed."

President Arabar agreed with her comments then said that although those losses were administration disappointments, at this time it wasn't that important. He continued, "We've divided the country so strongly now in our favor that it doesn't really matter that they're gone. We are well on our way to turning the communist-socialist project into total reality. We now have at least 47 percent of the population totally in our pocket. All I have to do is keep the pressure on, and the other few we need to control everything is like eating mashed potatoes and gravy. It's automatic."

Curtain said those other few needed would be easy to win over by continuing to push more free stuff, or promises of more free stuff, at them. "Even the staunchest advocate of earning their way will not refuse the opportunity to get more if it's free. A selfish heart creates grappling hands if that carrot dangles before their eyes often enough."

Attorney General Hand said, "Counting over 95 percent of our people who make up about 13 percent of the population, and the growing number of Hispanics that we help come into the country illegally, our voting supporters are growing leaps and bounds by the day. And considering the growing dependent underclass we continue to create each month with price increases we will soon be where we want to be; voting for just going through the motions. Almost all votes will be in our pockets before the polls open."

Harrett interrupted, "We're not there just yet. We haven't turned everyone into voting zombies just yet." She continued to explain there were still two problems they had to overcome. One was voter apathy; and to counter that the president had to remain more active to convince those people who had become complacent that it was still their responsibility to keep those greedy white rich people from cheating them. "They still must be convinced that they must fight for their rights, for what's fair."

"Melanie's right," Arabar agreed. "We're too close now. We can't afford to let up. We can't afford to let too many citizens come together in a common cause - that outdated concept they used to call 'patriotism.'

"Nobody cares about that anymore," Hand interjected. "During the last four years we've trained most of them to come to the door and beg for their free stuff. That concept of real patriotism is as outmoded to them as the Edsel automobile." He paused before he added, "And, during my conversation with the secretary of education, just yesterday, he told me our school project is progressing along with our other social policies."

"What do you mean?" Harrett asked.

Hand explained his conversation with that cabinet secretary, Carney Hines. During that very private conversation, Hines revealed their long time program of ridding those thoughts of patriotism and love of country were being replaced by more of their ideologies of how to keep the country as separated as possible. "Hines revealed he has gone to the Bible for guidance and reference to do that. For example, in those places they can find something to directly oppose, that's their new guidance to teach."

Arabar asked, "Did he give you any examples?"

"We talked at some length, and he mentioned a few things. One example he cited was somewhere in Chapter 20 of Leviticus where it said, "If a man lies with a male as with a woman, both of them have committed an abomination." Hand grinned as he continued, "That's our clue to destroy this once patriotic cohesive society. We just teach our children opposite from what it says in the Bible and our mission is pure and simple. It never fails."

Henry Carlton, the secretary of defense, said, "Our Defense Department is now going along with that idea. We've implemented the new homosexual cohabitation laws directed by the president, and with that preconditioning in schools, we've had no problems or complaints from those who once would have considered that an insult to their profession - once it would have been considered an abomination especially in the military."

Harrett said those military people had no choice. Even those who would object or complain about that policy would never say anything about it. "They know they must comply with orders of their superiors who must follow orders of the president. They live in a totally controlled society where they must keep their thoughts to themselves, and keep their mouths shut."

Carlton added, "If they say anything or do anything against that policy they know we will punish them, mark their record as criminal, and kick their asses out of the military." He looked at Arabar before he added that as labeled criminals and misfits, they would never find a good job or have a successful career, and they know it. "They know they can't screw around with us."

"I think we've already conditioned enough citizens to accept that abomination as normal," Grapalo exclaimed, "but

I don't think that's enough to totally digress or destroy a cohesive society."

Hand said Hines had told him something else about biblical guidance to further divide a society to expedite their total control. "He said something about trust and respect among citizens mentioned in Proverbs, Chapter 6."

"Did he explain what that was?" Harrett asked.

"Yes, but I didn't remember everything he said. Later I looked up that reference he gave me. It was in Verses 6 through 19."

"And--" Harret replied.

Hand said they were already doing most of the things that Proverb reference said was not acceptable to the Lord. "I guess that means things that would not be acceptable to keep a society together." He said that included haughty eyes, a lying tongue, hands that shed innocent blood, a heart that devises wicked plans, feet that make haste to run to evil, a false witness who breathes out lies, and one who sows discord among brothers.

"I'm not sure I agree with most of those prohibitions," Harrett rebutted. "Most of those things are what we just do - it's considered politics. We must sow discord to keep society separated, and we must tell a little white lie occasionally to make our point. Just look at how well the president sows discord by keeping our society so separated - the rich against the poor, the whites against the blacks and Hispanics."

Arabar took a deep breath before he protested, "I don't necessarily agree with the 'shedding innocent blood' part. Of course, we would never participate in or condone such a thing as that."

Carlton sighed then quietly remarked, "Possibly with the exception of a few occasions. Some of our overseas drone strikes miss their marks and murder people who have never expressed harm against us, or dislike of America. They just happened to be in a place at the wrong time. Maybe that could be considered innocent blood."

Harrett rebutted, "Mister President, you shouldn't be held responsible for that. That must be considered just an ordinary casualty of war, not killing of innocent blood."

"What war?" Carlton asked.

"The war on terror," Harrett quickly responded.

Arabar cautioned her, "I've told you never to say that - I've cautioned all of you never to say that! We can never use that comment. I might need their support some day and it might cause the millions of Muslims throughout the world not to like me." He looked around the table at his advisors before he added, "We must never forget that all Muslims are peace-loving people who just want to be left alone to worship in their own way. They are not concerned about those who choose not to worship as they do." He smiled a little grin as he added, "I might need their support one day to bring peace to Israel."

"I'm sorry, Mister President, I got carried away for a moment and forgot. I forgot there are some things we must never admit - or even discuss."

"Speaking of keeping secrets, Mister President," Secretary Carlton said, "I'm still having a few problems with concepts and problems among my senior military people. It could become serious if the press were to ever get involved for more disclosure."

The president asked, "What's that, Carlton?"

"Well, Mister President, it's about the Benghazi thing. Some of my senior people are still complaining and asking why we ignored and abandoned our patriotic citizens we allowed to be slaughtered there." He looked at the others around the table before he timidly continued, "I still don't have a good answer for them. They refuse to accept the policy explanation that there was not enough time to organize things to get there in time to prevent the slaughter. They know better."

"I know - that's too bad. To avoid that question, I told nasuS to convince the world that attack was a spontaneous thing created by a rowdy crowd protesting a video. We even showed the video to be sure they saw it or heard about it. Obviously she didn't do it well, or said some words that were not convincing. Our arrogant citizens kept pushing for more answers."

The secretary timidly pressed for a better answer. He reiterated that many of his senior military people knew what was going on in Benghazi, and would have known that scenario they presented was not completely true. "Where the difficulty is for me in explaining to those people that we didn't know of the danger there beforehand, and could not react was our known plans for quick reaction units. We knew Benghazi was a dangerous place. Some ambassadors had already left because they knew of the danger. And, the terrorists were already flying their flags in the neighborhood proclaiming that as their territory."

"Dammit! Do I have to keep reminding everybody they are not terrorists? They're just a few disgruntled rabble-rousers doing some stupid things. They pose no serious long-term threat."

"But, Mister President," Carlton insisted, our military strategy has always been to have rapid-reaction teams in a known position such as this. We had teams on stand-by, and all our senior planners know it." He paused and looked at the others at the table hoping for their support. When they all lowered their eyes, he continued, "How can I explain that to them?"

"Henry, you don't have to explain that to them. I'm their commander-in-chief. If I say blue is green, or black is white, it's your duty and theirs to say 'yes sir' and then shut the hell up."

During the quietness that followed, as Carlton nodded his compliance, Harrett broke the silence by saying, "The president had a busy schedule. He was busy all that day, once on the phone with Secretary Carlton discussing that matter, then he had to prepare for his trip to Las Vegas. It was an important fund raiser he couldn't cancel." She looked at the president before she added, "Besides, as the president said, those four men getting killed was just a little bump in the road, when greater things are considered."

"That's right," Hand agreed. "A little setback like that shouldn't ruin the president's standing in that part of the world. If we had sent men in, it might have upset some of them. We have to keep them somewhat cooperative."

"Well, that's over and done," the president concluded. Soon, that will be long forgotten by those who are making a big deal about it now. If it doesn't disappear by itself, I'll create another more important distraction by turning the finance and taxing problems at them. Those Conservatives don't have enough guts to stand and hold their ground too long. I keep bashing the hell out of them until they give in and give up."

Harrett agreed with the president, "You've done it again and again, Mister President. They don't stand a chance against your persuasions."

"You're right, Harrett. Our voting base is getting so strong to support us, that they have no option. They know they will lose more votes if they don't openly agree that we must do more for the poor people."

The homeland security secretary, Grapalo said, "And, we continue to build that base every day. More and more people are coming north across the borders and we continue to help them find a way to vote. Even those who become difficult to verify, we make sure only those who have relatives they can influence remain in this country. It shouldn't be long until voting will be automatic; we won't even have to campaign - just open the voting doors."

Carlton said he had heard that some illegal aliens were slipping in from other than Central and South America. "I've heard that many are coming in from Iraq, Iran, Afghanistan, and even Libya." He asked, "What's that all about?"

Grapalo looked at President Arabar before she answered. The president nodded, so she continued explaining that it fit in with the president's overall plan to make America a better place for all people. "Things are moving too slowly for the president, so he advised me to help speed up the process. He said he must have more power to do things before his opportunity ran out."

Arabar interrupted, "Look, as you all know, our administration is in the best position to do more for more citizens in our country than any time in history. Even the beginning of America was biased in favor of rich white men, those who considered themselves the privileged few. They controlled everything so none of the common people, the hard-working common everyday people, had a chance to share the new-found wealth of America."

"We started a plan a long time ago to right this wrong," Harrett continued. "President Arabar was the one chosen to do this, and so far he has exceeded all expectations." She continued to explain that the plan by a few inspired leaders was to become so influential that America could be remade into something to benefit all people, not just the privileged few. "To do that, we had to first turn things upside down; to fundamentally change America. Soon, the oppressed of American society will be rewarded with their fair share for helping the president accomplish this great task. It's a shared plan of total equality."

Carlton shook his head as he showed uncertainty about the plan to transition peacefully and for many American people to meekly accept the fundamental changes still to come. From previous briefings and conversations he knew the plan was for the president to slip into total control of America before the time for the next election.

The plan was that there would not be another election. The president would remain in power for life, or at least for as long as he wanted to, or was allowed to by his puppet-masters. The hope was that if there were another election, the outcome would be predestined by overwhelming voters on his side - but anything could go wrong at any time with just one major slip-up. He knew the decision had already been made to take over even by force if necessary. After a long silence he looked at Grapalo from homeland security and asked, "What about arms and ammunition?"

"Well, as you know, our plan is that it won't be necessary. Everything seems to be going the president's way now. His followers are even beginning to actually worship him as their god. Nothing will change their minds, no matter what he does or says."

"Carlton's right," the president said. "We still must stick to our planned contingency just in case we need to use just a little forceful pressure to accomplish what we must. We must be prepared for everything." He paused and looked directly at Grapalo.

With the president's stare, she didn't hesitate to reply with the current status. She reported that her staff at Homeland Security had already completed most of the planned actions. They had already bought all the high-powered ammunition off the market to prevent purchase by citizens who considered themselves patriots who would as they claim, 'protect America's freedoms.' That included 1.4 billion rounds: 450 million rounds of .40 hollow-point military style, 200 million rounds of .223 rifle ammunition, and 176,000 rounds of .308 168-grain hollow-point boat tail (HPBT) sniper ammunition. She concluded, "Comparing that to our usage in the Afghanistan war, it's enough to last 20 years."

Arabar waited for Grapalo to continue. She didn't, she just looked at him with a curious question on her face. Finally, he asked, "And, what about weapons?"

She was hesitant, but finally answered, "Immediately after your reelection most serious weapons flew off gun shelves and out gun stores before we could gain control of them. And, after the school massacre, and more people felt we would tighten the ban on weapons, more quickly disappeared."

She looked at the attorney general before she continued, "It seems everyone is concerned about there being a total ban on guns. And, some must realize what's in store for them soon. People keep showing up at gun stores every morning to see if any new ones have arrived."

"That's our worst fear," Carlton added. Looking at the president he continued, "If your takeover doesn't go perfectly, the question of resistance might arise; everybody who can use a gun has a gun. The question is; will they use them?"

Arabar replied, "Let's hope not; let's hope the takeover can occur normally; enough people are willing to support me that it shouldn't cause a problem, especially a military action problem."

Harrett had been listening intently to all the comments. When the president paused she said, "Our military still has more guns and bigger guns. We also have the more deadly firepower in our aerial weaponry and artillery. Those idiots wouldn't stand a chance in hell to resist, if that would be their intention."

Grapalo continued her remarks concerning ammuntion, "We're continuing to maintain a domestic ammunition shortage. As the popular ammunition comes off the manufacturing lines we keep buying most of it. We allow just enough to trickle out so the public won't realize what we're doing. It might cause them to panic. And, since those gun-lovers enjoy their target practice they will soon create their own shortage."

Everyone stared at the president while they knew he was pondering a deep concern about that last report from Grapalo. He ended the long silence with a question, "What about the Russians and the Chinese?"

Secretary of Defense Carlton asked, "What do you mean Mister President?"

Arabar answered by saying the Chinese would be the first to react if American freedom fighters, or anyone else needed bullets. "Not only would that be an opportunity for them to sell more stuff, it would also be an opportunity for them to weaken us even further. Of course they would find a way to slip it in to people who would fire against us - just like drug cartels do now."

"And of course the Russians would make sure everyone has enough bullets to fight us," Harrett agreed. "They still hold that deep resentment against us for losing the cold war."

Attorney General Hand said the idea of actual armed conflict using the military forces posed another great question: would our military fire on armed civilians if ordered to do so? He continued, "We just banned large capacity clips under the ruse that many bullets aren't necessary for home defensive purposes. We distracted the public by leading them away from the idea of using a high-powered weapon to defend their country."

"You're right," Arabar agreed. "The more we can weaken their defenses the better position that puts us in. But, there are still many stubborn ones arguing against these new restrictions claiming their founding fathers warned against an anarchist government."

"Those people just don't understand that we are just trying to protect them in the long run - the big picture," Harrett said. "They don't seem to understand that someone must be in control to protect the planet, prevent global warming, to limit our resource abuse, and to stop the world population growth that will eventually overwhelm us."

The president agreed, "Absolutely; we must protect them from themselves - but many will not understand that. They will just claim I'm power hungry and want to be king or something as atrocious as that. We just want to do what's best for their future, and the future of the world."

Hand interrupted again, "I'm still concerned about weapons and the military. What if a real armed conflict occurs and our troops refuse to fire on those who would defy the government - anarchists?"

Arabar answered, "They would never do that. I'm the commander-in-chief. They would have to do what I ordered."

After the uneasy pause, Carlton asked, "Do you remember the last great change in Soviet politics? Boris Yeltzin, the man who represented democratic change, stared down the muzzles of guns pointed at him from Soviet tanks. The Soviet military had been ordered to put down Yeltzin's followers. The tanks never fired their shells. The Russian military refused to fire on their fellow Russians, then had Yeltzin join them in a victory dance on those very tanks ordered to blow him away."

Harrett said, "Too many people love and worship our president. They would support him if the president urged them to. Surely, they wouldn't refuse to support him, as did the Russians."

"Well, considering that possibility," Arabar asked, "what's the status of our other contingency plan?" He waited for Grapalo's answer.

"Mister President, we still have several thousand military weapons, including those AK-47s from 'Fast and Furious,' hidden near the southern borders. We also have plenty of ammunition for those weapons as I indicated before." Before she continued she asked if it were appropriate to discuss more with the others present. He nodded, and she continued.

"The government in Venezuela continues to be very cooperative, since the transfer of funds from Brazil to them is functioning smoothly. No one has even imagined many of those funds allocated for oil development in Brazil is helping support our training camps in Venezuela. The Iranians and others training there believe they are being trained and equipped to return to Iran as freedom fighters. At the moment they don't have a clue of their real purpose, if that becomes necessary."

"And—what about the others who have already graduated from those training classes?"

"They are being infiltrated into inactive cells in our major cities until they're needed. Most still have not been told of their ulterior purpose. They think they're waiting to return to their home countries equipped as freedom fighters. We are supporting those with government transfer payments who can't find jobs while they wait.

Carlton interjected, "If what you suggest happens that might cause complications - you know, with our military people."

Arabar quipped, "I will have our military status so weak by that time, if it were to happen - if it were necessary - that they wouldn't be able to respond. Besides, we still control the equipment even if we can't control their ideas."

Carlton countered, "But it's still a dangerous prospect to consider, Mister President."

"Maybe we can keep the foreigners on standby out of it anyway," Grapalo suggested. "If our military were to become a problem because of foreigners we could just resort to the Homeland Security forces who would support us."

"How many American citizens now own guns?" the

president asked.

She said she didn't know, since every gun was not registered. "Besides, families have passed down guns for generations. There could be two or three in most households, as far as we know."

"Making gun registration should have been our first priority when I took office." He sighed, "I'm not sure we could even accomplish that now. Too many Americans suspect our actions, and would never report them anyway."

Carlton asked, "What if every American citizen owned a gun and was prepared to use it to defend their American principles?"

Arabar replied, "Maybe we should just focus on taking over through the political process first. Our first immediate goal must be to take over both houses of Congress with convincing margins. And, all I need is one or two more Supreme Court members in my pocket. That way we can do what I want, and it will seem the natural American way planned by our Founding Fathers."

"Is that possible?" Carlton asked.

"More and more are coming around to our way of thinking. As long as we keep promising more free stuff and more of their fair share, more keep rushing to vote for us."

Harrett exclaimed, "Just think; being elected a king with a democratic vote! Who of our founding fathers could have even imagined that?"

Something to note:

In his 'Call to service' speech July 2, 2008 in Colorado Springs, then presidential candidate Barack Obama said, "We cannot continue to rely on our military in order to achieve the national security objectives we've set. We've got to have a civilian national security force that's just as powerful, just as strong, just as well-funded." What did he mean by that? What would be the purpose of that civilian national security force? He has never explained, but recent events suggest he is beginning to act on that plan he revealed during that speech.

Recently, the Department of Homeland Security, operating under strict Obama policies has bought 1.6 billion (that's billion - with a B) rounds of high-powered ammunition, 7000 full-auto assault rifles, and 2700 armored vehicles. There's still some uncertainty about the vehicles, but The Department of Homeland Security has not revealed the purpose for the other weaponry.

Is it to be used against drug smugglers crossing our southern borders? Is it to be used against radical Jihadists led by the ghost of Osama Bin Laden wading ashore at the Boardwalk in Atlantic City? Or is to be used against those rowdy grandmothers who don't win enough when they play 'Bingo' at the community center? Who are these weapons to be used against? Department of Homeland Security, just tell us an answer that makes sense. Our Founding Fathers spoke against a force such as this and said it would be dangerous to its citizens. Is it?

Chapter 8

BEYOND REVELATION

Many who read this book, and countless others throughout the world, despise the Bible and everything for which it stands and represents. Therefore, this chapter will have no meaning to them, only continued disdain. There are two references, however, that might help some of those lost souls take a different look at the meaning of prophesy. It's about things said two thousand years ago that could not have been understood until our modern age. John wrote these things in the Book of Revelation. How did John know this?

But for those few among us who still worship God and Jesus, there are a few things John wrote in the Book of Revelation that we will understand and respect. It's foretold there's nothing we can do to affect the outcome of events written therein; the option left to us is personal salvation. We must recognize the signs of the end times and be prepared. The Bible gives this warning at the beginning of Revelation, the very first chapter:

"The Revelation of Jesus Christ which God gave unto him, to shew unto his servants things which must shortly come to pass; and he sent and signified it by his angel unto his servant John;

2 Who bare record of the word or God, and of the testimony of Jesus Christ, and of all things that he saw.

3 Blessed is he that readeth, and they that hear the words of this prophecy, and keep those things which are written therein; for the time is at hand."

Will there be any doubt when He comes? Will He be confused with one of the antichrists? How will we know the difference? Verses 7 and 8 continue and make that answer very clear:

"7 Behold, he cometh with clouds; and every eye shall see him, and they also which pierced him; and all kindreds of the earth shall wail because of him. Even so, Amen.

8 I am Alpha and Omega, the beginning and the ending, saith the Lord, which is, and which was, and which is to come, the Almighty."

The question is: when will the ending begin to happen? Of course, that definite date does not exist and one would likely be considered a false prophet if he or she pretended to know that exact date or time, such as boarding a space ship following the Halle-Bopp Comet, as did Applewhite. However, there are many signs which signal the quick decline of humanity that grows larger before the ending.

At this time Barack Obama is at the forefront of much of that immorality and social decline. His leadership in this process is another indicator that the serpent he so proudly wears on his ring represents Satan, that old dragon often identified in the Bible. Many sins encouraged by Satan are stated in the Bible, but some are more clearly emphasized than others. Consider these and look around to see how often many of these are coming more commonplace in everyday life. These are many of those things John wrote about as transgressions and fornication. These things will also be magnified in the end times supporting the arrival of the antichrist:

> Leviticus 18:22, "You shall not lie with a male as with a woman; it is an abomination."

> Leviticus 20:13, "If a man lies with a male as with a woman, both of them have committed an abomination."

> Proverbs 6:6-19, "There are six things that the Lord hates, seven that are an abomination to him: haughty eyes, a lying tongue, and hands that shed innocent blood, a heart that devises wicked plans, feet that make haste to run to evil, a false witness who breathes out lies, and one who sows discord among brothers."

> Galations 5:19-21, "Now the works of the flesh are evident: sexual immorality, impurity, sensuality, idolatry, sorcery, enmity, strife, jealousy, fits of anger, rivalries, dissensions, divisions, envy, drunkenness, orgies, and things like these. I warn you, as I warned you before,

that those who do such things will not inherit the kingdom of God."

Romans 1:26-27, "For this reason God gave them up to dishonorable passions. For their women exchanged natural relations for those that are contrary to nature; and the men likewise gave up natural relations with women and were consumed with passion for one another, men committing shameless acts with men and receiving in themselves the due penalty for their error."

Proverbs 12:22, "Lying lips are an abomination to the Lord, but those who act faithfully are his delight."

How do these abominations and transgressions affect a nation and not just the individual who commits them? Leviticus 18: 24,27-28 explains:

"Defile not yourselves in any of these things; for in all these the nations are defiled which I cast out before you." "(For all these abominations have the men of the land done, which were before you, and the land is defiled;)" "That the land spue not you out also, when ye defile it, as it spued out the nations that were before you."

Finally, after reading this first part of Revelation many times it became clear why John's message to the seven churches in Asia Minor is so important and so relevant today, and to the end times described later in Revelation. It associates those transgressions and those abominations with the other events announcing the pending arrival of the antichrist, the beast, and his mark that requires absolute obedience and total turning away from the real God. It's a final reminder in the last book of the Bible that God will allow mankind to determine his own destiny - individually, and as a nation, and as a world. It's a choice, not a demand. But, the consequences will be to the land of the people as well as to the individual transgressor.

Barack Obama is at the forefront of many of these serious abominations and transgressions. One in particular - homosexuality. He openly and aggressively supports homosexuality, claiming it's a right guaranteed under our Constitution, although God specifically says homosexuality is an abomination. Nowhere in the Bible does it say homosexuality is a right, or is even right in itself. Perhaps Obama is supporting homosexuals to gain more sure votes in the future. But, why does he need more votes in the future? Supposedly, he's already serving his last term as president of the United States.

I've already proposed an answer to this question in the last chapter in the dialogue scenario. Barack Obama does not intend to give up his powerful position at the end of his current term, ending in 2016. How can he remain in power even if our Constitution says he can only serve two terms with ten years maximum? He can do it either one of two ways.

One way is to insure both houses of Congress become overwhelmingly Democratic. Having both houses supporting him and controlling the Supreme Court with his last two appointments he can either have the 22nd Amendment to the Constitution changed to allow him to run for another term, or even longer; or he can find a way to circumvent the Constitution that will not be challenged by either house of Congress. The Supreme Court is so stacked to support him that he would have no difficulty finding a Constitutional loophole to remain in power. Simply, he will continue to campaign instead of being a leader to support all Americans. He is too selfishly power driven to do otherwise. He is still campaigning hard to insure both houses of Congress will support him, no matter how unconstitutional his actions will become.

The greatest question is: is he seeking this power as a personal quest, or is he trying to position himself for a greater cause - such as the leader of a one-world system? Perhaps at this time he doesn't even know that answer himself. He is merely on a quest he doesn't understand that drives him to that time when the 'seven heads rise from the sea' to become one united world. A united world would require a one-world leader. Perhaps his destiny moves closer. Perhaps the serpents in his ring, that icon of the 'old dragon' will guide him to that destiny.

If his desire or natural urge is for more power, as is natural within all mankind, that urge can be commonly understood. That's the natural urge of greed the Bible warns against. It's something most people understand and control within their own sense of right and wrong, or in their honesty to conform to God's word. That part could be inborn within his deep personality. It could also be guided by his Muslim faith that he claims 'not' that demands certain things must be followed as dictated by those in position to do the dictating.

It's most likely that this drive for personal power is his natural inclination. However, the other possibility can't be totally discounted. Perhaps he could be following a plan by puppet-masters to create that 'New World Order.' We know what an autocratic government or a dictatorial government looks like. We've seen those come and go throughout history. The extremes go from much loss of life to total elimination of personal aspirations. Ordinarily, over time, those collapse. But what might a New World Order look like? At the moment, that could consider three different scenarios. When either of these occur, it could represent the 'end of times' mentioned in the Bible.

120

The first could be a simple autocratic world government with a figurehead, or with a group acting as a figurehead. This is the organizational structure ordinarily envisioned when the concept of a one-world government is discussed. Under this form, countries would still exist as separate entities socially and religiously, but with all political decisions made by the central government. Likely, religious differences would be tolerated so long as nothing in that religion interfered with the concepts and dictates of the central government. Of course, all military functions would be under the single authority and organization of the world leader. This would be to enforce dictates, and to prevent or discourage wars between assigned boundaries. Perhaps titles of those within assigned borders would be such as they were during the old Roman Empire; governor or proconsul.

Biblically, this could be the worst time for Israel. The leaders of Israel would have to make a serious decision; would they become a member of the new order? Or, would they have that option? According to Bible prophesy, this could be the time Israel is forced to agree to something they know might sign their death warrant. Perhaps Daniel 18: 23 and 25 gives a clue:

> "And in the latter time of their kingdom, when the transgressors are come to full, a king of fierce countenance, and understanding dark sentences, shall stand up."

> "And through his policy also he shall cause craft to prosper in his hand; and he shall magnify himself in his heart, and by peace shall destroy many -"

"And by peace shall destroy many." Perhaps that danger would begin slowly, such as signing a peace agreement to become a member of the world body to have access to world trade. Can you imagine a country completely cut off from imports or exports? Could a small country such as Israel provide itself with enough food, chemicals, mechanical devices and other raw materials to survive? They would have no choice if the world body made the decision to cut them off. This would be similar to the condition individuals would face in having to choose the 'mark of the beast' described in Chapter 13, Verses 16 and 17:

> "And he causeth all, both small and great, rich and poor, free and bond, to receive a mark in their right hand, or in their foreheads: And that no man might buy or sell, save he that had the mark, or the name of the beast, or the number of his name."

Then, once Israel signs that agreement to become part of the world order and accepts the policies therein, what if the world order demands Israel give up its defensive weaponry? Would Israel do that if that were one of the requirements for the world governing body to maintain peace between borders? If this were the case, and if Israel refused to abandon or destroy their protective weaponry we can only guess what might happen then. The Book of Revelation describes that possibility in gory detail.

Would the United States come to the aid of Israel at that time of its greatest need? Absolutely not. If Obama has his way, the United States will be no stronger than any other country at that time. As the Bible says, that's when the restrainer that protects Israel will be lifted. The 'beast,' the world leader at that time will be the first to lead the attack against Israel. It will be on the Plain of Jezreel, near the ancient site of Megiddo - the word that's forms the concept of 'Armageddon.'

Already one of Obama's great supporters and chief advisors has issued statements condeming Israel. Samantha Power even sits on Obama's National Security Council. She is extremely anti-Israel and suggests that Israel is the source of most problems in the Middle East. In an interview in 2002 she even said Israel should be invaded to force them to allow Palestine to set up a separate state. She also scoffs at the idea that Iran is planning to build a nuclear bomb to use against its neighbors, especially Israel.

It certainly wouldn't be in Israel's best interest to sign an agreement with a world governing body, if this person is sitting on a council there that could make a decision to invade Israel for lack of compliance with one of their rules. Certainly the leaders of Israel are aware that to sign any agreement with a world government would be to sign Israel's death warrant.

Perhaps to prepare for that possibility, that scenario, we should all read the Book of Revelation for more understanding. According to that scripture, Satan's great prize, the goal he seeks highest, is to sit on the throne of God, in Israel. Perhaps we should give the serpent with which Barack Obama so proudly adorns on his finger much consideration.

The next one-world option to consider is that which the Islamic world has threatened - or promised. Those who are most boastful claim they will convert everyone to Islam throughout the world or kill (behead) those who refuse to convert. They are not subtle about their plans. They openly shout it from the greatest halls of government. A strong clue to this possible scenario is given in Revelation, Chapter 20, Verse 4:

"And I saw the souls of them that were

beheaded for the witness of Jesus, and for the word of God, and which had not worshiped the beast, neither had received his mark upon their foreheads, or in their hands; and they lived and reigned with Christ a thousand years."

Radical Muslims seem to delight in beheading people who don't agree with them. In our modern culture the word 'beheading' is not commonly associated with any other cult, religion, or organization. Therefore, this reference would suggest that the beast and his followers would likely be Muslims. Otherwise, why wasn't the word 'killed' used in this reference?

Now, considering from a practical point of view, what known Muslim exists today that has the world stature to occupy the highest position on the planet? Not one. In fact, isn't it ironic that Muslims spend too much time fighting and killing each other to allow one known Muslim to ascend to a higher position? Much of their dislike of each other is power politics, but the fundamental internal hate is from their basic religious ideologies.

They are ideologically separated by a similar difference that separates Christians and Jews. One part, the Shiites, believe their Messiah, the Mahdi, has already arrived on earth and is just waiting for the right time to start leading them to create purity in all the world - thus the beheadings. The other part of Islam, the Sunnis, doesn't believe the Mahdi has arrived yet. Since this divisive concept was developed hundreds of years after Christianity appeared, it's likely it's a concept copied directly from the differences in beliefs between Christians and Jews. And, as with Christianity, there are even further divisions in each of the two major parts of Islam.

Although some die-hard Christians still hate Jews because they believe the Jews crucified the Messiah, generally Christians and Jews have a cooperative respect for each other. Regardless of their differences, Christians still respect the Jewish nation for being the fountainspring of Jesus. The Islamic world exhibits less tolerance to one another - or to anyone else who disagrees with them. If they don't have a good excuse to kill each other, they seem to be capable of inventing one.

At the moment no self-proclaimed Muslim is in a position to be recognized for consideration as a world leader. If as the Book of Revelation proposes, as suggested by the act of 'beheading,' then that leader, that beast, would likely be a Muslim-in-waiting, or a Muslim-in-disguise. There's only one Muslim supporter today, who claims not to be a Muslim, who occupies a position to fill that role, and who is exhibiting extreme ambition to do so. That person is Barack Hussein Obama. But who is this man? Does anyone really know - for sure?

Who is this man? Many in America are uncomfortable with his position as their leader - with the full power and influence of the position he occupies. They are aware that he has the power to fundamentally change their lives as he promised to do when he said he would "fundamentally change" America. Yet, many do not trust his origin, his development, or his goals.

What is the goal and purpose of someone who would fundamentally change the great qualities of the United States? For almost 250 years America has had great struggles and has had many good things and bad things happen to its economy, culture, and society. But, America has maintained the one great fundamental; freedom and democracy guided by our United States Constitution. To 'fundamentally change' something means to change the constitution of the foundation. To fundamentally change America is to destroy the Constitution that guides us, thereby meaning to destroy America.

That's what he promised when he first campaigned for

president of the United States. Many people followed him, trusted him, believed him, and agreed with him. That means his followers also wanted 'fundamental change' in America. In effect, they wanted to destroy America as it was established and still existed.

Certainly those followers didn't purposefully and willfully intend to destroy America and the idealism it represented with the change they envisioned. Obviously, most love America as much as those who looked at Obama and realized the danger he presented to our Constitution. Those who respect our Constitution, but followed Obama to the cliff of despair were mesmerized by his voice and his great words; they looked no further than the great presentation. They imagined only great things for themselves in the future. His great words were forecast in Revelation 13:5 and 6:

"And there was given unto him a mouth speaking great things and blasphemies. And he opened his mouth in blasphemy against God, to blaspheme his name, and his tabernacle, and them that dwell in heaven."

His worshipers saw not the future of the country. They saw only the imaginary utopia he promised them. He promised them their illusive 'fair share.' He failed to explain that a fair share includes the fair share of economic and cultural despair that often accompanies illusive dreams. They didn't question his promises. Instead, they were swept away by his rhetoric, believing he had all the right answers. But, did he? What are his principles and character?

How knowledgeable is Barack Hussein Obama? He presents himself as the knowledge fountain, and he claims he was born in Hawaii. If he really were born in Hawaii and lived there, certainly being a man of his self-proclaimed high intelligence he would know that Hawaii was the last state to enter the union of the United States. Hawaii was the fiftieth state. Yet, on one occasion in a large forum he referred to the fifty-seven states of the United States. Can you even imagine any novice politician would not know how many states comprise the United States? Yet, his followers continued to be dazzled by his "speaking great things," not by his knowledge foundation.

Of course, his mesmerized followers said he just forgot. But, along the way what if he forgets other things; things such as what is the historical foundation of our great nation and the historical value of our allies and friends throughout the world? What if he forgets that America's foundation was guided by Christian principles; not Islamic, Hindu, or Buddhist principles? What if he forgets that our American flag that has represented hope for millions of people around the world should be respected? What if he forgets that America might be the last great hope for mankind and he fails to protect that historical heritage?

Many of us who objectively watch and listen to his words and actions believe he has no real concern about the longevity or the future of our country. This man of such great knowledge, who speaks such "great things" obviously doesn't know many of these important things regarding America, such as freedom and democracy. Clearly, he is now leading us into a negative direction of biblical consequences.

Is he trustworthy and loyal? During his first campaign for president he initially proclaimed that Reverend Jeremiah Wright had been his good friend and mentor for over twenty years. Then came the video of Reverend Wright preaching from the pulpit, "No, no, no, not God bless America!" But instead, "God damn America!" After facing more political pressure, Obama claimed he had never heard Reverend Wright say anything like that or that he had never said anything against America. He even said something to the effect that he would no more throw his good friend and mentor under the bus than he would his grandmother.

Suddenly, Wright was no longer his good friend and mentor. Wright disappeared into the sunset wiping bus tire tracks off his face. Good friends? How does a loyal and honest person treat good friends?

Obama claims he hardly knew his good friend and party pal, Bill Ayers, the man who expressed his patriotism with bombs against America. He is also the man, along with his father, who is thought to have helped launch Obama's political career. What was the ultimate purpose? Was it to support Bill Ayers' continued hate and aggression against America?

He claimed to know Ayers only as someone he casually saw in the neighborhood. He failed to reveal that he was on two boards with Bill Ayers, the Annenberg Project and the Woods Foundation, and that on at least one occasion he attended a party at Bill Ayers' home. Why did he not tell the whole and revealing truth about his association with Bill Ayers? Why did he keep that information a secret even if it were a casual acquaintance or an incidental event? What was he afraid of? If he were that non-associated with Bill Ayers why did he not say so and reveal the whole truth? What were the hidden secrets? Does not a minor deception require more questions? This Ayers' relationship is analyzed further in a later chapter.

Does he dishonor and degrade America? Does he dishonor Christianity? Does he exhibit blasphemy when he shows subservience to another god? One act he made spontaneously suggests a 'yes' answer to these three questions.

On one major occasion, televised and broadcast, he demonstrated weakness and disrespect to the office of the President of the United States. Although the whole world watched as he bowed to the Saudi King, who represents the highest level of Islam, during his visit to Saudi Arabia, he claimed he did not bow to that king. This was another blatant dishonesty, one of many that he spewed from his lips. The whole world watched him bow to the Muslim king, on television, yet he had the blatant arrogance to deny that he did. Of course, those who worship him believe him, even if they witnessed the event themselves. They agree with him that he never did such a thing. This arrogance of Obama, and the blind worship of his followers is an event that approaches biblical prophesy.

For the moment let's just ask the question; who would bow in the presence of a Muslim leader - other than a Muslim? Certainly it must be someone who felt inferior to that person. Did Obama feel inferior because of world position, time in position, or because Obama himself is a Muslim of lower rank than the Saudi king? There was a reason. Obama never explained that reason. Apparently, he feels his worshipers love him so much he does not need to express a reason. They will just follow him over the cliff with their eyes closed - without questioning. In any case, his bow in subservience demonstrated disrespect to the status of the United States of America, and more importantly: blasphemy against God.

Two incidents mentioned earlier will be repeated here. They're so significant, for this discussion, they deserve a double-take:

"Would a Christian routinely blaspheme God, as Barack Obama continues to do? Other than those incidents already mentioned, another more blatant blasphemy occurred on April 16, 2009 by the Obama group.

On that date, Obama required the monogram, consisting of the letters IHS, for the name of Jesus, be covered before he made his speech at Georgetown University. The monogram above an archway was covered with black painted plywood. Certainly he would not consider this blasphemy - black painted plywood covering the symbol of

Jesus. Yet, on March 21, 2013, he proudly stood under a large background picture of Yasser Arafat - the 'Father of Islamic terrorism' - as he gave his speech to the Palestinians in Ramallah. Does that not boldly suggest his inclinations?

Obama was also recorded at a closed-door fundraiser in San Francisco making disparaging comments about religion. He said, "You go into these small towns in Pennsylvania and, like a lot of small towns in the Midwest, it's not surprising they get bitter, they cling to guns and religion or antipathy to people who aren't like them or anti-immigrant sentiment or anti-trade sentiment as a way to explain their frustrations."

His comment didn't specifically say 'Christians' but that's the dominant religion referred to in the Midwest. A reference that clinging to religion (Christianity) out of bitterness and frustration and not out of search for truth and salvation is another bold example of his common blasphemy against Christ and the Bible. So, which religion or group does Obama really support? Let's consider some of his close contacts. And, here's even more about Obama's Muslim connections and support.

An Egyptian magazine claims that six American Islamist activists who work with the Obama administration are Muslim Brotherhood operatives who enjoy strong influence over U.S. policy. The December 22nd story published in Egypt's Rose-El-Youssef magazine suggests the six turned the White House from a position hostile to Islamic groups and organizations in the world to the largest and most important supporter of the Muslim Brotherhood. Chapter 13 gives a deeper look at the Muslim Brotherhood to understand just how dangerous they are to Americans - and Westerners.

The six named people inlcude: Arif Alikhan, assistant secretary of Homeland Security for policy development; Mohammed Elibiary, a member of the Homeland Security Advisory Council; Rashad Hussain, the U.S. special envoy to the Organization of the Islamic Conference; Salam al-Marayati, co-founder of the Muslim Public Affairs Council (MPAC); Imam Mohamed Magid, president of the Islamic Society of North America (ISNA); and Eboo Patel, a member of President Obama's Advisory Council on Faith-Based Neighborhood Partnerships. (Keep ISNA in mind when you read Chapter 13.)

Alikhan is a founder of the World Islamic Organization, which the magazine identifies as a Brotherhood subsidiary. It suggests that Alikhan was responsible for the file of Islamic states in the White House and that he provides a direct link between the Obama administration and the Arab Spring revolutions of 2011.

Elibiary, who has endorsed the ideas of radical Muslim Brotherhood luminary Sayyed Qutb, may have leaked secret materials contained in Department of Homeland Security databases, according to the magazine. He, however, denies having any connection with the Brotherhood. He also helped define the Obama administration's counter terrorism strategy, and the magazine asserts that Elibiary wrote the speech Obama gave when he told former Egyptian President, Hosni Mubarak, to leave power.

According to the magazine, Rose El-Youssef, Rashad Hussain maintained close ties with people and groups that it says comprise the Muslim Brotherhood network in America. This includes his participation in the June 2002 annual conference of the American Muslim Council, formerly headed by convicted terrorist financier Abdurahman Alamoudi.

The magazine also reports that Patel maintains a close relationship with Hani Ramadan, the grandson of Brotherhood founder Hasan al-Banna, and is a member of the Muslim Students Association, which it identifies as a large Brotherhood organization.

Obama's continuing closer ties with the Muslim community, especially the Muslim Brotherhood, invites another more serious question regarding our potential physical security. Why is he sending more sophisticated weaponry and military support to them? At the moment it seems to be only to Egypt. He plans to send military F-16 aircraft to them soon. What next? And, which other Muslim Brotherhood countries does he plan to arm next? And, for what purpose?

He may refute the fact all he wants; but he has proven to be a Muslim. And, his propensities suggest he could even be a radical Muslim when his real intentions are clear and exposed. Is his destiny to become that one-world leader for which Revelation awaits?

This analysis about a one-world order controlled by Muslims is the second possibility. The third consideration is that proposed by Agenda 21, which will be discussed next.

Chapter 9

AGENDA 21

The third possibility or concept for establishing a one-world order is to conserve natural resources and protect the planet. There are those among us who believe they can control our planet more effectively than God. They just discovered global warming and think they should be masters of it. God has warmed and cooled the planet for millions of years and He probably has a pretty good handle on things.

For example, a few thousand years ago the world was so cold that snow and ice permanently covered the United States almost to Texas. Then it slowly started warming and the ice line moved farther northward. And, it's still moved closer to the Arctic Circle. It's happened before, then when God figured the time was right, he created another Ice Age. Sometimes He even flips things around and puts everything in different positions probably just to have a little fun. What was the seabed is now a high flat desert. What once was a mountain is now below the water.

I don't know if God does that just to have fun or for another reason; perhaps to keep the temperature on earth equalized over a long period of time; and perhaps also to counter the normal activity of erosion, that if left unchecked would make the earth totally flat and covered in water. Who knows why He does what He does, but I'm sure it's for a good reason. And, probably He does it much better than those who call themselves experts. Nevertheless, many seem to think they are smarter than God. So, they invented Agenda 21.

Al Gore, the man who discovered or invented global warming and the internet would be proud of ideas proposed in Agenda 21. Given enough time, I suspect years from now he will even be the one credited with inventing it, discovering it, or proposing it.

What is Agenda 21? The following is taken from online Wikipedia articles to define and explain. Since I have no first-hand knowledge or information about Agenda 21, I had to rely on other sources for an explanation. Most Americans, more than 85 percent have no knowledge of Agenda 21. It seems to be a socialistic and 'Big Brother' concept to the extreme.

Agenda 21 is a non-binding, voluntarily implemented action plan of the United Nations with regard to sustainable development. It's a product of the UN Conference on Environment and Development (UNCED) held in Rio de Janeiro, Brazil, in 1992. It's an action agenda for the UN, other multilateral organizations, and individual governments around the world that can be executed at local, national, and global levels. The '21' in Agenda 21 refers to the 21st century. It's been affirmed and modified at subsequent UN conferences. 'Agenda 21' is a 300-page document divided into 40 chapters that have been grouped into 4 sections.

Section I: Social and Economic Dimensions. This section is directed toward combating poverty, especially in developing countries, changing consumption patterns, promoting health, achieving a more sustainable population, and sustainable settlement in decision making.

Section II: Conservation and Management of Resources for Development. This includes atmospheric protection, combating deforestation, protecting fragile environments, conservation of biological diversity (bio-diversity), control of pollution and the management of biotechnology, and radioactive wastes.

Section III: Strengthening the Role of Major Groups. This includes the roles of children and youth, women, NGOs, local authorities, business and workers, and strengthening the role of indigenous peoples, their communities, and farmers.

Section IV: Means of Implementation. This implementation includes science, technology transfer, education, international institutions, and financial mechanisms.

What are NGOs as stated in Section III above? They are non-governmental legally constituted organizations created by natural or legal people that operate independently from any form of government. The term originated from the United Nations and normally refers to organizations that are not a part of a government and are not conventional for-profit businesses.

In the cases in which NGOs are funded totally or partially by governments, the NGO maintains its non-governmental status by excluding government representatives from membership in the organization. The term is usually applied only to organizations that pursue wider social aims that have political aspects, but are not openly political organizations such as political parties. The number of NGOs operating in the United States is estimated at 1.5 million. Russia has about 277,000 and India is estimated to have had around 3.3 million NGOs in 2009, just over one NGO per 400 Indians, and many times the number of primary schools and primary health centres in India.

The UN Department of Economic and Social Affairs Division for Sustainable Development monitors and evaluates progress, nation by nation, towards the adoption of Agenda 21, and makes these reports available to the public on its website.

Australia, for example, is a signatory to Agenda 21, and 88 of its municipalities subscribe to ICLEI, an organization that promotes Agenda 21 globally. Australia's membership is second only to that of the United States. Opposition to Agenda 21 in Australia is not covered in the major media outlets though groups such as Act Australia, a 'fringe' political organization, has labeled Agenda 21 a "threat to freedom". European countries generally possess well documented Agenda 21 statuses. France, whose national government, along with 14 cities, is a signatory, boasts nationwide programs supporting Agenda 21. Like Australia, however, some opponents have expressed that they view Agenda 21 as a "sham."

In Africa, national support for Agenda 21 is strong and most countries are signatories. But support is often closely tied to environmental challenges specific to each country. For example, in 2002 Sam Nujoma, who was then President of Namibia, spoke about the importance of adhering to Agenda 21 at the 2002 Earth Summit, noting that as a semi-arid country, Namibia sets a lot of store in the United Nations Convention to Combat Desertification (UNCCD). Furthermore, there is little mention of Agenda 21 at the local level in indigenous media. Only major municipalities in sub-Saharan African countries are members of ICLEI.

Agenda 21 participation in North African countries mirrors that of Middle Eastern countries, with most countries being signatories but little to no adoption on the local-government level. Countries in sub-Saharan Africa and North Africa generally have poorly documented Agenda 21 status reports. By contrast, South Africa's participation in Agenda 21 mirrors that of modern Europe, with 21 city members of ICLEI and support of Agenda 21 by national-level government.

The United States is a signatory country to Agenda 21, but because Agenda 21 is not a treaty, the Senate was unable to hold a formal debate or vote on it, nor was it ratified by the executive branch. Several congressmen and senators, however, have spoken in Congress in support of Agenda 21; these include Representative Nancy Pelosi, then Senator John Kerry, and Senator Harry Reid.

In the United States, over 528 cities are members of ICLEI, an international sustainability organization that helps to implement the Agenda 21 and Local Agenda 21 concepts across the world. The United States has nearly half of the ICLEI's global membership of 1,200 cities promoting sustainable development at a local level. The United States also has one of the most comprehensively documented Agenda 21 status reports.

Reportedly, during the last decade, opposition to Agenda 21 has increased within the United States at the local, state, and federal levels. The Republican National Committee adopted a resolution opposing Agenda 21, and the Republican Party platform stated that "We strongly reject the U.N. Agenda 21 as erosive of American sovereignty." Several state and local governments have considered or passed motions and legislation opposing Agenda 21.

Activists, some of whom have been associated with the Tea Party and some other news organizations have said that Agenda 21 is a conspiracy by the United Nations to deprive individuals of property rights. A poll of 1,300 United States voters by the American Planning Association found that 9% supported Agenda 21, 6% opposed it, and 85% thought they didn't have enough information to form an opinion. Below is an article originally published in Eco-Logic Online in 1997:

"In communities across America, "stakeholder" councils are being formed, or have already been formed, to advance Agenda 21 to transform cities and towns into "sustainable communities." The consensus process is used to gain the appearance of public support for the principles of sustainability, applied to a particular community. The process is designed to take the public policy-making function away from elected officials and place it in the hands of non-elected officials, while giving the appearance of broad public input into the decision-making process.

Stakeholder councils are called by many names and are created for a variety of specific purposes. Whatever they are called, and whatever the stated purpose for which they are created, they all have several common characteristics, and all have a common objective: the implementation of some component of Agenda 21. While each community may experience a variety of different approaches, it is necessary to recognize the common principles that guide all such councils.

Objectives

The general objective of all stakeholder councils is to promote three primary values: environmental protection, equity, and sustainable economic development. To promote these values, a comprehensive community plan must be developed which links, or integrates, all three values. In some communities, stakeholder councils are formed to work on a single component of a comprehensive plan that is to be combined with the work of other councils that may be working on different components in different geographical areas of the same community. The various councils may or may not know about the work of other councils that is underway simultaneously.

Currently, the most common stakeholder councils are related to the visioning process to create "Sustainable

Communities;" Ecosystem Management Plans, Heritage Area or Corridor Plans, River Protection Plans, Biosphere Reserves, and Economic Renewal Plans. Almost always, the plan will encompass more than one political jurisdiction. In some instances, several counties and states may be included, as in the case of the East Texas Ecosystem Plan, which embraced 73 Texas counties and a small portion of Louisiana. In other instances, the plan may be confined to a single county or city. When a plan focuses on a single town or county, someone, somewhere, is planning to incorporate that plan into a multi-jurisdictional plan.

The stated purpose of the stakeholder council may be related to environmental protection only, which is usually referred to as natural resource management. It could be related to any one of several other single subjects such as economic renewal, education, emergency response, or transportation. Or, the stated purpose could be to develop a comprehensive plan that addresses all the issues. Whatever the stated purpose, it will attempt to integrate environmental protection, equity, and sustainable economic development.

The Process

Stakeholder councils do not simply appear. Nor are they formed as the result of citizen response to a common problem. Someone creates them - with great care. They could be formed by a government agency, or by several government agencies working together; they could be formed by NGOs (non-governmental organizations) or by a combination of government agencies and NGOs - which is often the case.

The Environmental Protection Agency and several other federal agencies offer grants to NGOs and local government agencies as incentives to create these councils and develop plans to achieve sustainable communities. Whoever instigates the process will carefully select individuals from the community to participate in a meeting, which will evolve into a series of meetings. The individuals selected will be chosen because they are known to share philosophical objectives, and to represent broad segments of the community. The poor, disabled, indigenous populations are specifically targeted. Representatives from government agencies are also targeted. Typically, at least one elected official from each of the political jurisdictions in the plan area is invited. Someone from industry, and a landowner or two are also among those invited.

Formation of the original group is extremely important. People who support the objectives of the originators must dominate the group. There also has to be an appearance of broad community representation. The original group may be quite small, or it could be quite large, depending upon the objectives and the size of the community and the plan area. The initial meeting is rarely advertised. Participants are invited personally, and frequently hold several meetings before the press or the community is ever informed. By the time the public becomes aware of the existence of the stakeholders council, it is pretty well organized and its work is well underway.

The Techniques

The Consensus Process - often called "collaborative decision-making" - is a process that usually begins with a predetermined outcome. The agencies or NGOs that assemble an Ecosystem Management visioning council, intend to establish an ecosystem management plan. The originators know what they want included in the plan before the first meeting is ever scheduled. Those who assemble Sustainable Community visioning councils intend to establish a plan to achieve their vision of a sustainable community. The literature will say that broad community input is sought. In reality, the outcome has been decided before the first meeting begins; the real purpose for the process is to "educate" the participants.

A trained facilitator will conduct the meetings. A

consensus-building meeting is vastly different from a meeting conducted by Robert's Rules of Order. In a consensus-building meeting there are no votes. There is no debate. The idea is to avoid conflict and confrontation between and among differing views. The facilitator leads the discussion with questions that are skillfully crafted to elicit no response. Questions are framed to force respondents to disagree with a statement with which most reasonable people would agree. For example, a facilitator might ask: "Is there anyone who would disagree that we have a responsibility to leave future generations sufficient resources to meet their need?" Obviously, no reasonable person can disagree with such a statement. Silence - no response - implies that a consensus has been reached on the need to protect resources for future generations. The example is an oversimplification, but it illustrates the technique used by the facilitator.

Despite the careful selection of the participants, the facilitator may encounter an individual who does disagree with the questions. The facilitator is trained to marginalize such an individual by making him or her look silly by asking another, even more extreme question, such as: "Surely you are not telling this group that you feel no responsibility to your grandchildren, are you?" With such tactics, one who objects or disagrees very often is quickly labeled as a troublemaker and is either ignored or excluded from the group.

Eventually, a professional will write a report. It will be "The Plan," or the document produced by the group. Regardless of what the group's stated purpose may be, the final document will include language that says the plan is designed to integrate ecology, equity, and the economy; environmental protection, equity, and sustainable development.

The Players

The players will include federal, state, and/or local

government appointed officials. Working hand-in-hand, there will also be one or more representatives from NGOs that may or may not be recognizable. The Nature Conservancy and the Sierra Club are two of the more active NGOs instigating these stakeholder councils. Frequently, however, a new NGO will be created expressly for the purpose of instigating a stakeholder council in a given community. One or more of the larger NGOs, or an organization such as the Tides Foundation, will supply the start-up money and send a couple of professionals into a community to create an NGO such as "Friends of Hollow Rock, Inc." or something similar. Sometimes an existing local NGO will be used, with substantial financial and leadership help from a larger NGO, or with help from the federal government through one of the many grants that are available for the purpose.

Whenever it is possible, a well-known local figure - a politician, businessman, or landowner will be created to be the spokesperson. Such individuals give credibility to the process and can have enormous persuasive power over local residents.

With such a cast of players, using techniques that are skillful to the point of deception, in a process designed to produce a predetermined outcome, it is little wonder that the objectives of Agenda 21 are being implemented in cities, towns, and across the countryside of America. Those who recognize the inherent dangers in allowing non-elected bureaucrats to develop public policy, and those who can see the socialistic underpinnings of a managed society in the objectives of Agenda 21, need to rise to the occasion to stop the underpinning of the United States Constitution."

More About Agenda 21

This is a headline advertisement from Siemans: "Sustainable cities: Intelligent traffic solutions, green buildings, water management, and smart grid infrastructure are just a few of the technologies helping to steer today's urbanization toward sustainability."

The article from Siemans continues:

"The challenges presented by sustainable urban development are immense. In 2010, 82 percent of Americans lived in cities; by 2050 it will be 90 percent. Cities are responsible for around two thirds of the energy used, 60 percent of all water consumed and 70 percent of all greenhouse gases produced worldwide.

Sustainable cities are looking at ways to improve their infrastructures to become more environmentally friendly, increase the quality of life for their residents, and cut costs at the same time. With the world's most comprehensive environmental portfolio,Siemens is a perfect partner in sustainable city development. Our longstanding expertise has given rise to innovative technology for sustainable solutions in energy efficient buildings, water treatment facilities, transportation infrastructure, public safety systems and healthcare imaging and diagnostics."

Below is a blog at Infowars.com by Michael Snyder, on December 24, 2012 regarding Agenda 21. It's titled: Economic Collapse. It begins, "Agenda 21 is being rammed down the throats of local communities all over America." the article continues:

"Have you ever heard of Agenda 21? If not, don't feel bad, because most Americans haven't. It is essentially a blueprint for a 'sustainable world' that was introduced at the UN Conference on Environment and Development in Rio de Janeiro, Brazil in 1992. Since then, it has been adopted by more than 200 countries and it has been modified and updated at other UN environmental summits. The philosophy behind Agenda 21 is that our environmental problems are the number one problem that we are facing, and that those problems are being caused by human activity. Therefore, according to Agenda 21 human activity needs to be tightly monitored, regulated and controlled for the greater good. Individual liberties and freedoms must be sacrificed for the good of the planet.

If you are thinking that this sounds like it is exactly the opposite of what our founding fathers intended when they established this nation, you would be on the right track. Those that promote the philosophy underlying Agenda 21 believe that human activity must be 'managed' and that letting people make their own decisions is destructive and dangerous. Sadly, the principles behind Agenda 21 are being rammed down the throats of local communities all over America, and most of the people living in those communities don't even realize it.

So how is this being done? Well, after Agenda 21 was adopted, an international organization known as the International Council for Local Environmental Initiatives (ICLEI) was established to help implement the goals of Agenda 21 in local communities. One thing that they learned very quickly was that the Agenda 21 label was a red flag for a lot of people. It tended to create quite a bit of opposition on the local level.

As they try to implement their goals, they very rarely use the term 'Agenda 21' anymore. Instead, they use much more harmless sounding labels such as 'smart growth', 'comprehensive land use planning' and especially 'sustainable development.' So just because something does not carry the Agenda 21 label does not mean that it is not promoting the goals of Agenda 21.

The goals of Agenda 21 are not only being implemented in the United States. This is a massive worldwide effort that is being coordinated by the United Nations. In simplified terms, Agenda 21 is a master blueprint, or guidelines, for constructing sustainable communities. Agenda 21 was put forth by the UN's Commission on Sustainable Development, and was adopted by over 200 countries (signed into law by George Bush Sr.) at the United Nations Rio Conference in 1992. In 1994, the President's Council for Sustainable Development was created via Executive Order by Bill Clinton to begin coordinating efforts at the Federal level to make the US Agenda 21 compliant.

The same year that Bill Clinton established the President's Council for Sustainable Development, the International Code Council was also created. The International Code Council has developed a large number of international codes which are intended to replace existing building codes all over the United States. The following is a list of these codes:

International Building Code

International Residential Code

International Fire Code

International Plumbing Code

International Mechanical Code

International Fuel Gas Code

International Energy Conservation Code

ICC Performance Code

International Wildland Urban Interface Code

International Existing Building Code

International Property Maintenance Code

International Private Sewage Disposal Code

International Zoning Code

International Green Construction Code"

(Note: how many other codes and codifications will be enforced through agreements like these. The one most in question is gun control laws. The greatest desire of our current national and international leaders is to ban all guns - except theirs. Once that happens 'Big Brother' will have no one to challenge his every whim.)

In summary, it seems Agenda 21 is an idea or a plan in 'outer brainopia' to put the conceived needs of trees, grass, sunshine, oil, grasshoppers, fleas, spiders, wind, rain, and anything that exists on, below, or above the earth on a higher concern than the concern for people. Perhaps at its most extreme, Agenda 21, or its more all-inclusive term 'sustainable development,' would require mankind to yield all to nature. It would finally achieve that great Orwellian dream of a place of 'Utopia.' No one would have to worry about anything because it would all be distributed equally to everyone who lives there. Those in Brainopia would develop and control that paradise, Utopia. For those who have not heard, this is the concept from which 'Big Brother' was derived.

Perhaps I should slip back into my fiction role to give an example of what this inspired condition of sustainable development might be like. Although the concept of Agenda 21 is for there to be no direct leaders, only organizers and monitors, can you in your wildest dreams imagine that not happening? Wanting to be in control and the drive for more power is a natural lust for those guided by Satan, and there are many more being guided by Satan as more and more move away from God each day, as they are deceived by the 'man of voice who speaks great things.'

So, for this example, let's assume President Arabar, with his world presence, conspires to gain this control. How might that happen, and what would happen next? Let's begin with another cabinet meeting, only this time it's at the world level, somewhere in Sweden or Norway. This leader should also be somewhere in Europe to deal with Israel, in case Israel decides not to play their world game - at their peril. The Bible suggests that final attack upon Israel will have an old Roman Empire origin.

The Scenario

President Arabar was initially accepted into his position as world leader with the title, Chairman. He didn't really like that title that had just emerged from his central involvement, but decided to use it until he gained more control. He didn't want to seem too kingly or emperor-ish too soon.

He waited for the ten leaders from all seven continents to get comfortable in their seats before he began. He had to show a little restraint anyway, initially, because these leaders hadn't been formally elected by citizens. They had just informally assumed control with their many contacts within the sustainable development programs. Real elected officials had been ignored and left out of the process. What regular citizens thought about their plans wasn't important.

He began, "I'm glad everyone made it on time today. I was a little concerned because I didn't know if the fuel allocation for each of your aircraft had been scheduled on time. I see the scheduled 'just in time' allocation worked."

The South American governor, Juan Hernandez replied, "I was concerned at first, because I couldn't really order the pipeline and fuel supply people to set aside that much fuel for my trip. Usually, they produce just enough for emergency needs. Everyone tries to stick to the guidelines that any unnecessary fuel exhaust will do that much more damage to our planet. Fortunately for me, someone else had not used their allocation."

Arabar responded, "I guess we need to do something about our necessities. Since we are the ones our people look to now to get things done, perhaps we should assume more direct control. We must get an organized system in place."

Jesse White, the North American governor, echoed the comment from Hernandez and said he couldn't get fuel for his flight until the very last minute. "It's much more difficult when you have to beg and scheme to get your needs fulfilled. It will be so much better when we have enough direct power that's recognized so we can make the right decisions up front."

"Well, gentlemen," Arabar said, "perhaps we can solve that problem right now. We must have organization; we must have someone in charge so we can get things done. We don't want things to get out of control as they were before; with each little geographical area running on its own. Each area must be programed for its best and highest use to conform with needs of our planet and atmosphere."

Hussein Brenka, the Middle Eastern coordinator, not yet having assigned himself the title of governor, complained, "Things are still moving too slowly in my region. I can't get everyone together to cooperate in their zones. Most still want to keep everything separated. The imams want their own little groups and they continue to be more influential in their growing areas, the chieftains still think they are in charge of their provinces, and even the elected officials act as if they should have some say over how we plan things for their overlapping areas. They keep everything so personal and have no shared sense of responsibility."

"Perhaps after the conclusion of our meeting - if we all agree- we can take care of some of those problems that still hamper our goal of making everything on earth more sustainable. Each region must understand there must be more personal sacrifices to produce the maximum results from the dwindling resources of our planet."

Brenka responded, "I can't really get much done in my area until I have some kind of real authority. I can only suggest, and get some of my people to just move into certain areas. I think those who would oppose us are now unsure of their power status."

"With all my volunteers in all the crevices of government, I pretty well control things in Africa," Hector Muzamba reported. "Since we're not too thickly populated, many people across borders already assume I'm a higher appointed authority." He smiled before he continued, "No one questions it when I introduce myself as 'governor or facilitator.'

"Yes," Arabar replied, "I understand your areas are progressing very well."

"It hasn't been difficult to train and mold those people. Most believe what we are doing is natural and necessary. They especially like the idea of communal cooperation. Most have been relocated into dispersed pockets of larger urbanization. I've convinced most that living closer together in high-density high-rises saves time and resources, and allows more land to be used for cultivation."

Arabar urged, "Of course you are aware that areas used for cultivation must be within walking distance of those urban centers; at least close enough that people can get to their fields on bicycles?"

"Of course. We started that part of Agenda 21 ten years ago. Keeping within those guidelines, the nearby areas are used for dairy and farming. Distances further than that are left idle to allow reforestation of the planet. We must have more trees and wild vegetation to reduce carbon dioxide and increase the amount of oxygen in the air."

Jesse White said, "I thought most of the oxygen came from the oceans."

"We can't publicize that," Arabar replied. "We must have that reason to keep the population communalized for a more important reason; to stop global warming and to save the planet."

Hussein Brenka waited for a long silence before he spoke, "Clustering more people into more concentrated urbanized zones also allows us another important function; religious purity. Allowing people to be too spread out to distant locations allows us less control. They can wander about expressing their own thoughts and ideas. Allah does not allow that."

"You're right, Hussein," Arabar agreed. "But, we shouldn't dwell on that too openly now. We should wait until our brothers gain more control over more of the world with our silent Jihad. We still have time, a hundred years or more if necessary."

"I disagree with you somewhat, Mister Chairman. The longer we allow this free expression and lack of respect for our religion to continue, it creates a greater problem. Too many of these women today act like they are the same as men. That situation continues to grow as we have to stand silently by and do nothing about it." Hussein looked deeper into Arabar's eyes and added, "Now, I don't know how much trouble I will have with some laws if I beat some of my wives. This is an intolerable situation for us."

"I understand that," Arabar consoled Hussein, "but, we have to wait until we have more concentrated areas where it will be easier to take control. Now, people with too many different ideas are too widely dispersed, and many of them still have guns; guns powerful enough to fight back."

Jesse White, from North America, said, "Certainly, that's the major reason we're having to move so slowly and cautiously in the United States. Too many people own guns, and not many are registered so we can track them down. If we make an open show of force, we don't know what would happen. Perhaps a real uprising would reveal our plan."

"Of course you're right, Jesse," Arabar agreed. "I understand that even little old grandmothers who are suspicious of our ideas are arming themselves - and even going to ranges to learn how to shoot."

Hector Muzamba interrupted, "That's what you get for allowing average citizens to own guns. Just imagine one of Brenka's fearless Jihad fighters armed with an AK-47 being blown away by a little old grandmother with a shotgun. That would be insulting."

Hussein asked, "How many weapons are in the hands of average American citizens?"

Arabar looked at Jesse White and waited for an answer.

"That's the most dangerous part for us," White responded. "We don't have a clue. If we move too quickly we wouldn't know where to look for safety."

Arabar replied, "That's the problem with that Constitution. It made it more difficult for us to bring real structure and progress to the world. We don't know what those people are really thinking - or how far they would go to keep what they keep calling, 'real freedom.'"

White concluded, "I'll keep stressing that problem on the elected leaders when I get back home. Perhaps I can convince them to institute more gun free zones, then when we get everyone moved into the communal pods the gun free zones can be assumed to exist as we move people in. They will have to surrender their weapons at the gates, or they will be discarded into the uninhabited areas."

Arabar agreed that would be a simple process, and would only take a few years. "Of course, all the elected officials must be convinced - at first - until citizens come to rely only on our requirements as they come into the system."

Hernandez asked, "What system is that? I missed the last meeting, and perhaps I missed that part."

"At our last meeting, we all agreed that we must bring everyone together so we can conform to the strict rules we need to protect the planet. Carbon based energy sources must be totally eliminated and replaced with more environmentally friendly sources - such as solar and wind."

"I thought we were having a problem with developing those power sources," Hernandez replied. "Wind is too unreliable, and solar is not powerful enough to support everybody. To enforce those measures fully would require different societal measures - very extreme. People seem to want to stick to their modern conveniences."

"And, we'll get to that position eventually," Arabar exclaimed. "But, that might take as long as a decade or so." He paused and carefully added, "But we are already planning our first firm steps to get to that position."

Muzamba said, "Juan, at the last meeting we all agreed that our sustainable development movement, Agenda 21, already had enough social and environmental controls that we can essentially bypass those elected officials who are not fully behind us. Already, in Africa, we are seen as the ones making things move along. We haven't been challenged with our plans to move everyone into close-knit communal groups to maximum our natural resources. And, we are setting the example in population control."

"What do you mean by population control?" Hernandez asked.

Muzamba glanced at Arabar before he answered, "No one questions abortions anymore. They are accepted whenever they're needed to reach the level of sustainability." He paused and looked longer at Arabar before he added, "And, it seems there's always a medicine shortage for a person after a certain age."

Arabar interrupted, "Of course that age will depend on the maximum sustainable population quota at any certain time or event - such as a time of severe drought, or another natural disaster."

Hussein added, "Those old people are gonna die anyway. Why should we keep them going that much longer to cause pain to the more productive people, and waste our limited resources, like in that movie, 'Soylent Green?'"

"I'm still not totally clear on that part, myself," White said. "How can we get enough people dedicated to support programs like that? That's never been part of human culture and understanding."

Arabar explained that it would be a relatively simple system to apply and enforce. First, would come a system of dedication, where anyone who agreed with the system and wanted to be part of it would be recognized as a loyal member who would abide by all the rules and requirements. In return for that loyalty and dedication to the system, they would be the only citizens allowed to transact business - buying and selling.

Hernandez asked, "But, how is that possible? How could it be controlled?"

"That's the most simple part," Brenka answered. We just assign everyone a special personal number - then load that and other information into a tiny computer chip. Then the chip can be implanted into anyone's hand."

Arabar continued the explanation, "With a RFID chip implanted in everyone, money will no longer be necessary. The chip can be used as a simple debit card. When someone buys or sells something the transaction will be recorded on the master computer. Of course, only those who accept the program would be allowed to have the chip."

"What would happen to the other people, if anyone doesn't agree to support your program?" White asked.

Brenka answered, "Our people are certainly prepared to deal with anyone who refuses to be part of this program. It's too essential that everyone cooperates to protect the planet and help make the world a better place." He glanced at Arabar before he continued, "We already have our armed cells in place to deal with any of those people who would be deemed 'terrorists' by the organization. I can just turn my people loose and they will take care of those things."

"You don't have enough armed people to take care of all the terrorists, rebels, and dissenters who would still be roaming around out there trying to act independent," Hernandez said. "How would you deal with those?"

"We already have enough control over the few remaining military forces, and some of our followers in the Homeland Security group to take care of those scattered about in more isolated places." Arabar continued, "And, we have made great strides in our drone programs to eradicate those trouble-makers who will exist at the time of the great transition - and any who would attempt to isolate themselves after they have accepted the mark of the chip. We already have small solar craft that can lounge over an area indefinitely watching for any suspected rebels. It's a simple matter of pushing a tiny button to fire the necessary shot from that drone."

Hernandez agreed, "It would take only a few months to have the system totally purged and clean."

They all sat compliantly for a moment until Arabar interrupted the stillness. He asked, "Okay, we need to formalize this organization before we leave here today, so we can assume the direct power. What effective name should we give our organization? What should be our titles; what should my title be?"

Chapter 10

THE END TIMES

According to the Bible's Book of Revelation, two people will emerge near the end of time who will lead the world into a cataclysmic event. This time is often called the apocalypse, and just as often it's called Armageddon. In either event, this time is considered the time the world will end. But, exactly how that ending will occur no one is certain. Many Christians believe the earth will end, and the new earth will be the one in Heaven. Others believe the ending is only symbolic and a new and more peaceful world will continue, ruled by God.

The 'Battle of Armageddon' is to take place near the ancient site of Megiddo, which is the basis from which the word Armageddon is derived. Megiddo overlooks the Jezreel Valley. This is the likely site of the final great battle. Other elements of the battle also suggest the war events will take place on a broader scope involving nuclear, chemical and biological weapons

The Book of Revelation says two major events will occur regarding the beast, often called the antichrist; the false prophet, often called the second beast; and Satan. This is also confusing to some people. Simply stated: the false prophet will be a supporter and promoter of the beast. The beast is usually called the antichrist. When the world gets so bad, and when Israel is attacked, the Lord will throw the false prophet and the beast down into the deep fire pits.

When He disposes of those two, then the Lord and the souls of those who were beheaded for refusing to worship the beast, and refusing to accept his mark, will reign for a thousand years. The beginning of this thousand years many people believe an event called the 'Rapture' will occur. This is when they believe real Christians will be raised up to Heaven before the 'bad' events occur. The word 'Rapture' is not in the Bible. The only ones to be raised up to reign with Jesus are the soul of those beheaded. No one will escape those horrible end times - only those dedicated souls.

At the end of those thousand years, often called the Millennium, the Lord will return to earth to dispose of Satan, that old dragon, the same way he did the false prophet and the beast, that antichrist. The mystery is what happens to the earth when Satan is disposed of. Most Christians believe the earth will be obliterated and only the souls of those whose names are in the 'book of life' will be with the Lord in Heaven.

Although Satan gives the antichrist his power when the one-world government is formed, when those 'seven heads rise from the sea,' clearly many people must be fooled, deceived, to follow him and worship him. This is the job of the false prophet, to promote the antichrist, and prove he is worthy of worship. He will promote the antichrist as Christ on earth. Let's analyze his function first.

According to the Book of Revelation another person will appear toward the end time who will support and promote the antichrist, the first beast. He will be known as the second beast, or the false prophet. He will be part of what's termed the 'unholy trinity.' GotQuestions.org gives a description of this person:

"The apostle John describes this person and gives us clues to identifying him when he shows up. First, he comes out of the earth. This could mean he comes up from the pit of hell with all the demonic powers of hell at his command. It could also mean he comes from lowly circumstances, secret and unknown until he bursts on the world stage at the right hand of the antichrist. He is depicted as having horns like a lamb, while speaking like a dragon. The horns on lambs are merely small bumps on their heads until the lamb grows into a ram. Rather than having the antichrist's multiplicity of heads and horns, showing his power and might and fierceness, the false prophet comes like a lamb, winsomely, with persuasive words that elicit sympathy and good will from others. He may be an extraordinary preacher or orator whose demonically empowered words will deceive the multitudes.

Verse 12 gives us the false prophet's mission on earth, which is to force humanity to worship the antichrist. He has all the authority of the antichrist because, like him, the false prophet is empowered by Satan. It is not clear whether people are forced to worship the antichrist or whether they are so enamored of these powerful beings that they fall for the deception and worship him willingly. The fact that the second beast uses miraculous signs and wonders, including fire from heaven, to establish the credibility of both of them would seem to indicate that people will fall before them in adoration of their power and message. Verse 14 goes on to say the deception will be so great that the people will set up an idol to the antichrist and worship it."

Ever wonder why John's vision that produced the Book of Revelation has been so difficult to understand in the past?

As we get closer to the basis for his vision, many things are becoming more clear, and make more sense if taken in context of modern times. Two verses in particular are more relative to today's happenings than they were when they were first written. In these verses, John is speaking of this second beast, that false prophet, who is the supporter and promoter of the first beast, the antichrist. This second beast is believed to be a religious man. At one time in the past, many even believed it was the Pope. Let's look at that ancient information in terms of our modern times:

> Chapter 13, Verse 13, "And he doeth great wonders, so that he maketh fire come down from heaven on the earth in the sight of men."

This was to prove to people that he was a messenger from God and was endowed with great powers. Therefore, people should believe him when he proclaimed how great that god, the antichrist, was and they must worship him.

Two thousand years ago when John had that vision from Christ he had no idea what to call missiles and rockets. He saw streaks of fire trailing missiles and rockets and didn't know how to precisely describe what he saw. And, during John's vision of the Apocolypse, there's no mention of Jesus explaining the vision, only showing it. John had to explain it the best way he saw it.

John probably knew that to call it bolts of lightening would not be accurate, so he simply called it fire. If he had described it as bolts of lightening he was probably aware that description could have referred to other Roman and Greek gods of that time, such as Zeus and Thor. Zeus was still a great recognized god of that time.

Logically, fire was a generic description. In our modern world, we know that many rockets and missiles leave a trail of fire. Now, we even have the beginning of laser weapons that could be called fire coming from the sky. This description fits more with our modern times than during the time of John.

And, even more recently we hear of drones that already have amazing capabilities. Isn't it conceivable that very soon a small camouflaged drone could hover overhead, unseen, and send fire down to earth, even aimed at targeted people who refused to worship the beast? That aerial platform, drone, could be so small and unseen that it would appear fire was falling from heaven. And, considering even further; couldn't a laser beam or a missile be targeted to a specific RFID chip implanted in someone's hand - that 666 mark of the beast so often mentioned? These end times could be danger beyond our wildest imaginations. Perhaps John interpreted this fire as miracles rather than a forceful military action.

> Chapter 13, Verse 14, "And he deceiveth them that dwell on the earth by means of those miracles which he had power to do in the sight of the beast; saying to them that dwell on the earth, that they should make an image to the beast, which had the wound by the sword, and did live." (According to both Christian and Muslim writings, the first beast (the antichrist) and the Mahdi had been injured.)

> Chapter 13, Verse 15, "And he had power to give life unto the image of the beast, that the image of the beast should both speak, and cause that as many as would not worship the image of the beast should be killed."

Two thousand years ago, John likely had never seen a

keyboard, a computer, or a hologram. Even if he saw those things in his vision, how would he have explained them at that time - other than the way he did? The image was a computer that could speak. So what? Many computers and their little wired or wireless friends speak to us now, everyday. We also have the internet, a world-wide system that can speak to anyone in the world. This is likely the way the 'mark of the beast' will be applied, enforced, and controlled. Verses 16 and 17 explain the use of that master computer, the image of the beast:

> "And he causeth all, both small and great, rich and poor, free and bond, to receive a mark in their right hand, or in their foreheads: And that no man might buy or sell, save he that had the mark, or the name of the beast, or the number of his name."

This information would have been a cryptic puzzle to John, and to those of that time who read his writing. Anyone today can easily see how these applications can be applied. Most are already active, even today in our everyday lives. We have social security numbers, driver's license numbers, credit card numbers and many other ways to be identified. According to the verses above, we will accept another central world number saying we worship the beast - or we will be killed.

The mark in their foreheads might have a different meaning than as it's simply stated. In other places in the Bible a mention of a mark in their foreheads of Christians, simply means that they have accepted Christ. There's not necessarily a physical mark present. Perhaps John's intention was to give this important clue only two verses later, directly below the Chapter 13 verses, shown above. Chapter 13 has only 18 verses. Immediately, the first verse of Chapter 14 states:

> "And I looked, and, lo, a Lamb stood on the mount Sion, and with him an hundred forty and four thousand, having his Father's name written in their foreheads."

This same statement might apply equally to worshiping the beast, that antichrist. This would suggest that a mark in the right hand would be an actual physical mark, or an object such as an RFID chip that might be used also as a credit card or debit card to "buy or sell."

This Chapter 14 reference is also the one that many believe suggests that 144,000 Jews will convert to Christianity before the end times. That belief is from the words "having his Father's name written in their foreheads." That's different from saying "His" name written in their foreheads.

Perhaps this is the right time or opportunity to offer a thought to those who do not believe in Christ or God, or any of that 'religious stuff.' Of course, the Bible is full of wonderful stories and examples of faith; it's also full of horrendous events and tragedies; and it also has many examples and scenes that might cause one to really question the purpose for the Bible.

After all these past ideas and examples are considered, there is one place in the Bible that's current. It should make a non-believer ask, "How did John know that? John is looking at current events taking place right under our noses today. It would have been impossible for John even in his wildest imagination to envision what he is writing. These are the verses that show the transition between what has happened and what will take place when Armageddon begins. These verses have already been posted, but I will put them all together here, from Revelation 13, 11-18:

> 11 And I beheld another beast coming up from out of the earth; and he had two horns like a lamb, an he spake as a dragon.
>
> 12 And he exerciseth all the power of the first beast before him, and causeth the earth and them which dwell therein to worship the first beast, whose deadly wound was healed.
>
> 13 And he doeth great wonders, so that he maketh fire come down from heaven on the earth in the sight of men.
>
> 14 And deceiveth them that dwell on the earth by the means of those miracles which he had power to do so in the sight of the beast; saying to them that dwell on the earth, that they should make an image to the beast, which had the wound by a sword, and did live.
>
> 15 And he had power to give life unto the image of the beast, that the image of the beast should both speak, and cause that as many as would not worship the image of the beast should be killed.
>
> 16 And he causeth all, both small and great, rich and poor, free and bond, to receive a mark in their right hand, or in their forehead:
>
> 17 And that no man might buy or sell, save he that had the mark, or the name of the beast, or the number of his name.
>
> 18 Here is wisdom. Let him that hath understanding count the number of the beast: for it is the number of a man; and his number is six hundred threescore and six."

I put this information here because many people don't own a Bible and wouldn't have access to this information. This handy modern reference should be kept within easy access when the tendency to ask the question of one's personal salvation arises for those who are on the brink of believing. Although John does not realize the names of these things he reveals, he's describing aircraft, missiles, rockets, lasers, computers, keyboards, wireless communications and holograms. In the beast's mark he is also describing credit cards, WIFI systems and RFID chips. That should be enough to cause even the deepest non-believer to ask, "How did he know that - 2000 years ago?"

Furthermore, taking advantage of these non-believers in the end times are the deceivers, many are great deceivers. Although the term 'great deceiver' is never used in the Bible, there are, nevertheless, many of them out in the world trying to peddle their wares - of deception, so they can gain more control and become more powerful. For example, First Timothy, 4: first verse says, "Now the Spirit speaketh expressly, that in the latter times some shall depart from the faith, giving heed to seducing spirits, and doctrines of devils."

Perhaps these 'doctrines of devils' were on display at the 2012 Democratic National Convention. At that assembly was Barack Obama the 'seducing spirit' that led that group to depart from the faith?

In the Bible, God says many times He will turn His face from a country that turns its back on Him. Does the denial of God three times at the Democratic National Convention in 2012 again demonstrate this turning away by Obama and his party? Were they turning their backs on Him? This denial three times happened once before.

At the Lord's Supper, Jesus told Peter that he would deny Jesus three times before the rooster crowed. Jesus was arrested that night, and as he had said, Peter denied knowing

Jesus three times before the rooster crowed. Jesus looked Peter in the eyes as the rooster crowed. Peter wept in an action titled, The Repentance of Peter.

Isn't it ironic, and prophetic, that God's name was denied three times at the Democratic National Convention? Not once, not twice, but three times the convention members, by voice vote, chose not to include God's name in the party platform. When they were asked to affirm the name, most shouted 'no' or 'nay.' After the third vote, the chairman falsely claimed that the vote had been two-thirds in the affirmative, and God's name and the recognition of Jerusalem were put back in the platform. This is the source reference:

http://www.youtube.com/watch?v=aG6qgSfaARE

Was the prophesy by Jesus regarding Peter a hidden message about how God would be rejected at a later time? Was Peter used as an example to warn of humankind's modern-day denial of God? Why was God's name removed from the platform, the Democrats' ideology, in the first place? What pressure and from whom was someone forced to take that action? Only one man had enough power and authority to force that omission. Obama got caught, and his blasphemy against God was exposed. That blasphemy continued on the convention floor and was tolerated and repeated by his followers. Barack Obama had already made his denial of Christ known with his previous announcement, "America is no longer a Christian nation."

How many of his followers outside the convention are influenced by this Pied Piper of deceit also to reject God? Peter showed his repentance. Has there been any repentance from any of Obama's followers on the convention floor, or elsewhere? After he bowed to a Muslim leader in honor and reverence, he then says America is no longer a Christian

164

nation. Many of his actions and words continue to blaspheme God, and discredit the United States of America.

In several places in this book, I have already listed many of his blasphemies and his deceptions that lead others to follow him - to even worship him as Christ, returned. The most recent example that Obama should be loved was a comment rebutting one of my blogs at my Authorsden blog site. In it I criticized Obama. This was the comment from someone who took issue with my criticism on March 5, 2013:

> "I am sure that you are aware that the things you are writing are simply not true. So I believe you are do exercises in fiction writing and I don't think that is wrong.
>
> The seat of Satan can not be Barack Obama. You are looking too far - or better still you are merely influenced by your terrible lack of love for your president.
>
> As a retired army officer you should know truth and reality matters. The moment you lose focus of telling the truth God leaves you on your ways."

This writer lives in Kenya, so his word context is slightly off, but that's not a problem. My Kenyan would be much worse. And, the idea that he disagrees with my writing neither is a problem. I'm taking such a strong approach that I expect much strong disagreement. The part that concerns me is the comment about 'love.' I wonder if the word 'love' is too common among Barack Obama's followers. Perhaps those who agree with him and his policies should respect him. I think the term 'love' takes it to a level closer to worship. (As a matter of note: I'm a retired Air Force officer, not Army.)

I emphasized this comment above to demonstrate that

this blind passion for a leader is dangerous. It could be biblical. 'Deception' and 'blind followers' are mentioned many times in the Bible. The first time was at the very beginning of the Bible in Genesis 3: "Now the serpent was more subtle than any beast of the field which the Lord God had made." In this description, subtil was the word for deceptive. The first act in the Bible was deception by the serpent, Satan. That act has been multiplied many times, and according to the Book of Revelation exists even greater today. And when we speak of a deceiver in the Bible we generally refer to the beast, the one considered the antichrist. But, who could this person be when he is given his great authority by that dragon, Satan?

Many sections throughout the Bible give glimpses, traits, and hints of his identity. This is a listing of many of those, briefly stated:

He will be empowered by Satan, when Satan chooses.

He will first rise to power over 3 nations, then 10.

The 10 nations will be from the old Roman Empire.

He will be 'diverse' from the rest.

He will be a popular figure throughout the world.

He will blaspheme God.

He will be a man of 'voice,' a great speaker.

He will be attractive and charismatic.

From an injury, he will appear to be resurrected.

Initially, he will bring Israel unto a world covenant.

He will influence the rebuilding of the Jewish temple.

He will declare he is God in that new temple.

By his 'lying signs and wonders' many will believe

him.

The beast will not attack Israel until he has enlisted ten countries from the 'north' to create the invading army. Perhaps he has not reached the shores of Europe, maybe as the leader of the European Union or the United Nations, to create that condition, at least not yet.

In the past, most researchers who tried to interpret the actions and places of the 666 beast were stymied with the idea that the beast would lead countries from the north to attack Jerusalem. It's assumed those countries of the north would be those that once were part of the Roman Empire. But, from the north? How could that be?

A generation ago, that would not even have been conceivable. Now, that possibility has exposed itself to reality. Many things according to Revelation are becoming more visible in these later years.

What once was the dominant Christian religion and culture of Europe is fast being infiltrated and replaced with Islam and Islamic culture and traditions. How soon will it be before the Muslim population is large enough to politically control those once great European nations? Then the antichrist is likely to show himself.

The beast will be a man of great stature, of great voice, from an unknown origin, who will be loved by millions of followers. The beast most likely will be a Muslim. Who else wants to 'wipe Israel from the face of the earth?' The exception might be that he is not formally a Muslim, but is a Muslim sympathizer for political purposes. Let's use a for example.

For example, Barack Obama is recognized as a great orator, and his home of origin remains questionable. He has a percentage favorability rating of 92 in France, 89 in Germany, 73 in England, 71 in Spain, and 69 in Italy. And, that's before more Muslims continue to flow into those ten northern countries and convert them into their Islamic culture - as they openly boast they intend to do.

On at least three occasions, Barack Obama said he is a Muslim. Also, several official documents show his religion as Muslim. Regardless of what he officially claims, after living in Indonesia, the largest Muslim following in the world, how can he claim not to be a Muslim? And, we can't forget that 'mark of the beast.' And, we should not forget that Indonesian serpent ring he so proudly adorns on his finger. After reading John's warning to the church at Pergamum, could Obama's ring represent 'where Satan sits?'

Understanding these things, it's time to consider the next Bible reference: Revelation 13:18. This is the most identified and quoted verse in the Book of Revelation, The Apocalypse. John wrote:

> "Here is wisdom. Let him that hath understanding count the number of the beast: for it is the number of a man; and his number is Six hundred threescore and six." (666)

Scholars have long tried to interpret those numbers by association with the Greek alphabet. Would someone trying to tell us something that important create a cryptic puzzle too complicated to understand? Let's simplify John's information: "count the number of the beast for it is the number of a man;"

John said count; he didn't say interpret. If we count 6+6+6, the answer is 18. Now, let's say the beast's name will have 18 letters. That's counting; it's what John said to do. Now, use your imagination to picture a possible candidate of our time who has 18 letters in his full name. Surprised? One name fits perfectly.

BARACKHUSSEINOBAMA

We also have the confirmation of that number with a password. John must have had a sense of humor or intended a double check entry to make sure he was understood, even at the age of a hundred. Was his 6+6+6 equals 18 a joke, or was it an intentional answer to the great puzzle that John put this information in Verse 18?

Obama's Ring: The Seat of Satan

Chapter 11

THE SILENT JIHAD

Earlier in this book I mentioned that it's hard to find a specific target to defend against in an attempt by evil forces determined to destroy our great nation, America. At any instant in time, it seems the Socialists-Communists are forcing their hand upon our government and society. And when many of us turn our ideas to that line of defense others rise up. We are also concerned about radical Islamic terrorists who either sneak into our midst or whose ideas are changed in those among us who also spew terror from the face of evil.

Most recent research and indications are that now the greatest threat to our nation, our future, and our humanity is from the silent jihad that's flowed upon us. Too many indicators reveal that our current government administration is even part of that jihad against the intent of our Founding Fathers. No one in that administration will admit it or say it, so let's turn to a Muslim for that information.

The following comments are from an interview by Ryan Mauro, on RadicalIslam.org, with Salim Mansur, an associate professor teaching Political Science at the University of Western Ontario, London. Mansur is a Muslim:

Ryan Mauro: Can you give us a brief overview of what the struggle within Islam is like right now, especially in North America?

Salim Mansur: "I want to thank you, first of all, for inviting me to this interview for RadicalIslam.org as the organization's National Security Analyst.

The struggle within Islam in our time is between Muslims who embrace the values of the modern world in terms of freedom, individual rights, gender equality and democracy on the one side and Muslims who oppose these values and, hence, modernity on the basis of Sharia.

This struggle, therefore, goes to the very heart of how Muslims understand Islam either as a faith-tradition, or as a total system of belief and practice that is antithetical to the norms of the modern world. In other words, for Muslims who embrace modernity, as I do, Islam is a matter of personal belief and not a political system; and Muslims opposed to modernity view Islam ideologically, hence Islamism, and accordingly they embrace the views of Maudoodi and Hasan al-Banna, Syed Qutb and Khomeini, about Islam as a totalitarian value-system.

The seeds of this struggle or, more appropriately, the basis of conceiving Islam ideologically and in terms of politics and power might be traced back to the earliest years of Islam and Muslim history. But it is in our time, beginning in the middle years of the last century, Muslims have had to face the challenge of modernity when Muslim societies became independent states following the end of colonial rule by European powers.

This is a complex story. Let me note here only the following. The Muslim states sociologically speaking are almost without exception mostly poor developing countries wherein is found just about every aspect of under-development.

Despite the few states of the Middle East possessing petro-wealth, Muslim societies are relatively backward culturally, politically, technologically, and Muslims, in general, are denied freedom by those in power and who use Islam as an ideological instrument in legitimating their authority.

This is the Islam – as a totalitarian value system, as an instrument of authority and power, as a political ideology – presented as "unchanging," "true," "genuine" and "authoritative" by Islamists, and any Muslim questioning this "Islam" is considered a heretic or, worse, an apostate.

This is the Islam or Islamism of Maudoodi, al-Banna, Syed Qutb, Khomeini and their followers, such as Yusuf al-Qaradawi, the prominent Egyptian and Qatar-based exponent of Islamism.

Muslims opposing Islamism reject the Islamist view that Islam is unchanging, that the Qur'an is a closed book and not open to interpretation other than the Islamist version that builds upon, or extends, the interpretation made during the early centuries of Islam and turned authoritative by those in power.

Moreover, Muslims opposing Islamism are in many, if not all, instances anti-Sharia, and opposed to the political parties or movements associated with Maudoodi (the Jamaat-i-Islami in South Asia), with al-Banna and Syed Qutb (the Muslim Brotherhood in the countries of the Middle East and North Africa), with Khomeinism (the Shi'i version of Islamism in Iran and among Shi'i Muslims in the Middle East and elsewhere), and with Wahhabi-Salafi version of Islamism espoused by the Saudi Arabs.

The anti-Islamist Muslims are, however, vulnerable to Islamists and persecuted within the Muslim world as they lack political power or some support from those in authority, while they are mostly alone outside the Muslim world.

This struggle between Islam and Islamism, between anti-Islamist Muslims and Islamist Muslims, is the core struggle among Muslims at the present time. It takes many different forms given the vast diversity inside the Muslim world. It is also the much postponed, or stalled, movement for reform of Islam and the Muslim world analogous in many ways to the long and complex conflicts waged within Christendom and spread over several centuries through Reformation and Counter-Reformation that eventually culminated in the making of the modern world.

From a longer historical perspective this struggle within Islam was unavoidable, inevitable, and necessary as Muslims individually and collectively decide how to reconcile their faith with modernity. In this respect the present struggle raging among Muslims is not unique, since people of other faith-traditions – Christians were first – at different times struggled similarly.

The intensity of the struggle between Islam and Islamism can be assessed by observing the nature of Muslim against Muslim violence, and despite how beleaguered anti-Islamist Muslims are their resistance to Islamism is a compelling story of our time. The eventual outcome of this struggle, I believe, will have salutary effects for Muslims and non-Muslims in our increasingly interdependent world with the painstakingly difficult reform of Islam.

It is only in the midst of freedom and democracy found in North America that anti-Islamist Muslims can make their case, give moral support to anti-Islamists in the Muslim world, expose the nature of politics that make for such deplorable and, ultimately, evil alliance as that between the United States and Saudi Arabia, and question the West's support for governments in the Muslim world that are more or less opposed to the values of freedom, individual rights, women's equality, equal rights for and protection of minorities, and the norms of democracy.

But the lack of support for anti-Islamist Muslims in the media, and by government and non-government agencies, has meant in a cruel twist of politics that the most virulently anti-Western Muslims, the Islamists, are mostly listened to and their views receive undue attention in the making of public policy in respect to the Muslim world or individual Muslim states, in reporting news about the Muslim world, and in the prevalent dominant narrative about Islam.

Hence, the irony that North American institutions, government and non-government, instead of assuming the positive role of assisting in some measure the reform of Islam through support for anti-Islamist Muslims have done just the opposite, and frequently, by amplifying the voices of Islamists in the free world."

In summary, this is a Muslim saying what many Americans refuse to believe and refuse to admit. First, that there is an evil alliance between Saudi Arabia and America to promote Islam. Also that North American institutions are supporting and promoting the Islamists' (radical Islamists) point of view. If he can understand this dangerous situation and has the courage to say it, why doesn't our government have that much understanding and courage? Or, are they doing what they have planned to do for a long time. According to another document, this silent jihad started long ago, as revealed by the following document.

The 'Investigative Project on Terrorism' discovered a plan for the silent Islamic Jihad in America. The plan was written in May, 1991, and is titled: 'An Explanatory Memorandum On the General Strategic Goal for the Group In North America.'

This May 1991 memo was written by Mohamed Akram, a.k.a. Mohamed Adlouni, for the Shura Council of the Muslim Brotherhood. In the introductory letter, Akram referenced a "long-term plan approved and adopted" by the Shura Council in 1987 and proposed this memo as a supplement to that plan and requested that the memo be added to the agenda for an upcoming Council meeting. Appended to the document is a list of all Muslim Brotherhood organizations in North America as of 1991. These are some notable quotes from the document:

"Enablement of Islam in North America, meaning: establishing an effective and stable Islamic Movement led by the Muslim Brotherhood which adopts Muslims' causes domestically and globally, and which works to expand the observant Muslim base, aims at unifying and directing Muslims' efforts, presents Islam as a civilization alternative, and supports the global Islamic state, wherever it is.

In order for Islam and its Movement to become "a part of the homeland" in which it lives, "stable" in its land, "rooted" in the spirits and minds of its people, "enabled" in the live [sic] of its society and has firmly-established organizations on which the Islamic structure is built and with which the testimony of civilization is achieved, the Movement must plan and struggle to obtain "the keys" and the tools of this process in carry [sic] out this grand mission as a "Civilization Jihadist" responsibility which lies on the shoulders of Muslims and "on top of them" the Muslim Brotherhood in this country.

The process of settlement is a "Civilization-Jihadist Process" with all the word means. The Ikhwan must understand that their work in America is a kind of grand Jihad in eliminating and destroying the Western civilization from within and "sabotaging" its miserable house by their hands and the hands of the believers so that it is eliminated and God's religion is made victorious over all other religions. Without this level of understanding, we are not up to this challenge and have not prepared ourselves for Jihad yet. It is a Muslim's destiny to perform Jihad and work wherever he is and wherever he lands until the final hour comes, and there

176

is no escape from that destiny except for those who chose to slack. But, would the slackers and the Mujahedeen be equal."

The document also recommends that all the Muslim related organizations must be organized together under one banner for the common cause, and should work in the same spirit. That common cause is to "destroy America from within." Following is a partial list of those recognized organizations:

Islamic Society of North America (ISNA)
(reference page 131)

Established in 1981by the Saudi-funded Muslim Students' Association of the U.S. and Canada (MSA), the Islamic Society of North America (ISNA) calls itself the largest Muslim organization on the continent. ISNA was created by MSA with the help of one of Palestanian Islamic Jihad's founding students, Sami Al-Irian. Another noteworthy founding member of ISNA was Mahboob Khan.

Today ISNA's annual conventions draw more attendees, usually over 30,000, more than any other Muslim gathering in the Western Hemisphere. ISNA's mission is to function as "an association of Muslim organizations and individuals that provides a common platform for presenting Islam, supporting Muslim communities, developing educational, social and outreach programs and fostering good relations with other religious communities, and civic and service organizations."

ISNA focuses heavily on providing Wahhabi theological indoctrination materials to a large percentage of the mosques in North America. Many of these mosques were recently built with Saudi money and are required, by their Saudi benefactors, to strictly follow the dictates of Wahhabi imams; an edict that affects the tone and content of the sermons given in the mosques, the selection of books and periodicals that may be read in mosque libraries or sold in mosque bookshops, and the policies governing the exclusion or suppression of dissenters from the congregations.

Through its affiliate, the North American Islamic Trust, a Saudi government-backed organization created to fund Islamist enterprises in North America, the Saudi-subsidized ISNA reportedly holds the mortgages on 50 to 80 percent of all mosques in the U.S. and Canada. Thus the organization can freely exercise ultimate authority over these houses of worship and their teachings.

Writes Kaukab Siddique, the editor of New Trend, an Islamic periodical of extremist views that is nonetheless opposed to Wahhabi domination of American Islam: "ISNA controls most mosques in America and thus also controls who will speak at every Friday prayer, and which literature will be distributed there."

Islam scholar Stephen Schwartz describes ISNA as "one of the chief conduits through which the radical Saudi form of Islam passes into the United States." Adds Schwartz, "Our view is that the number of mosques under Wahhabi control actually totals at least 600 out of the official total of 1,200, while, as noted, Shia community leaders endorse the figure of 80 percent Wahhabi control. But we also offer a number of 4-6,000 mosques overall, including small and diverse congregations of many kinds."

According to Sufi leader Sheikh Muhammad Hisham Kabbani's testimony before a State Department Open Forum on January 7, 1999, extremists have taken over "more than 80 percent of the mosques in the United States. This means that the ideology of extremism has been spread to 80 percent of the Muslim population, mostly the youth and the new generation." Kabbani based his statement on his personal investigation of 114 American mosques. "Ninety of them," he said, "were mostly exposed, and I say exposed, to extreme or radical ideology, based on their speeches, books and board members." This is largely due to the efforts of ISNA.

According to terrorism expert Steven Emerson, ISNA "is a radical group hiding under a false veneer of moderation;" "convenes annual conferences where Islamist militants have been given a platform to incite violence and promote hatred" (for instance, al Qaeda supporter and PLO official Yusuf Al-Qaradhawi was invited to speak at an ISNA conference); has held fundraisers for terrorists (after Hamas leader Mousa Marzook was arrested and eventually deported in 1997, ISNA raised money for his defense); has condemned the U.S. government's post-9/11 seizure of Hamas' and Palestinian Islamic Jihad's financial assets; and publishes a bi-monthly magazine, 'Islamic Horizons,' that "often champions militant Islamist doctrine."

Muslim Student's Association (MSA)

The first Muslim Student's Association national chapter was formed in 1963 at the campus of the University of Illinois at Urbana-Champaign (UIUC) by international students. The initial leadership came from Arabic-speaking and Urdu-speaking members, with guidance from students of the Egyptian-based Muslim Brotherhood and Pakistan-based Jamaati Islami movements. A Saudi Arabian charity, the Muslim World League, provided early funding for the group. Early goals for the movement included the promotion of "a self-definition that involves initially and fundamentally an Islamic identity" of its members, as well as an appropriate Islamic lifestyle while they were in the US.

With time, MSA groups became more interested in seeking how to integrate and institutionalize Islam and Islamic culture into American life. Current issues such as the position of women in Islam and problems in the Islamic countries began to be debated. The groups proved important as mobilizers in developing increasing Muslim political activity in the United States. Student leaders, as these graduated, went on to form the Islamic Society of North America. From the 1960s onwards, the MSA engaged in educational activities, including the translation and publishing of works by major Islamic scholars. In 1966 MSA founded the Islamic Book Service, to distribute magazines and books. In addition, books about Islam were distributed on campuses to both Muslims and non-Muslims. In the 1970s, a fiqh, or legal council, was established by MSA; initially the fiqh rendered opinions on minor issues such as the start of Ramadan. By 1988, however, it was making decrees on a broad range of religious and social issues. The journalist Robert Dreyfuss in his book 'Hostage to Khomeini' described how the Muslim Student Association is just a front organization for the Muslim Brotherhood.

He also describes how Ibrahim Yazdi, the founder of the Iranian branch of the Muslim Student Association became one of the key supporters of Ayatollah Khomeini and served in the early government of the Islamic Republic. Robert Dreyfuss discusses how the Muslim Student Association has funneled money to various Islamic terrorist organizations .

Muslim Communities Association (MCA)

A WEST MIAMI-DADE, FL report: "Two prayer leaders, or Imams, from the Muslim Communities Association were arrested by federal agents on May 16, 2011, on charges of providing material support to the Pakistani Taliban and had their first appearance before a federal court earlier today. The court reset the detention hearing to next Tuesday.

Seventy-six-year-old Hafiz Khan, and his son, 24 year-old Izhar Khan, were taken into custody in Miami-Dade County and in Broward County, respectively. Both men, along with another son, 37 year-old Irfan Khan, arrested in Los Angeles, have been charged in a 4-count Indictment of sending at least $50,000 via wire transfers since 2008 to

180

family members in the Northwest Province of Pakistan. The elder Khan has also been charged with supporting the Pakistani Taliban, designated by the U.S. State Department as a terrorist organization, by running a school which also allegedly harbors Taliban fighters and allegedly trains children to become Taliban fighters.

Hafiz Khan is also a prayer leader at the Masjid Miami, also known as the Flagler Mosque, operated by the Muslim Communities Association. Izhar Khan is the prayer leader at Jamat Ul Mu'mineen Mosque in Margate, FL. Neither mosque nor any other member of the Muslim community have been implicated in the indictment. Wifredo Ferrer, the United States Attorney for the Southern District of Florida has emphasized that this indictment only names 6 individuals from one family, and does not involve and is not aimed at the Muslim community, the mosques, or Islam as a faith and culture."

The Association of Muslim Scientists (AMSS)

The Association of Muslim Social Scientists of North America (AMSS) says it was founded "by Muslim scholars with the mission to organize conferences that examine, debate and define Muslim perspectives on social issues of global concern." It is located in the same building as the International Institute of Islamic Thought (IIIT) and the Association of Muslim Scientists and Engineers.

The AMSS website states that it originated from the Muslim Students Association. The website states that those who founded it and the Muslim Students Association were also instrumental in establishing the Islamic Medical Association, the Association of Muslim Scientists and Engineers, IIIT and the Islamic Society of North America.

According to the investigation of these groups, every single one of these groups, including AMSS, is listed in the

1991 U.S. Muslim Brotherhood memo as among "our organizations and the organizations of our friends." The document states the Brotherhood's "work in America is a kind of grand jihad in eliminating and destroying the Western civilization from within."

Association of Muslim Scientists and Engineers (AMSE)

Popularly known as AMSE, the Association of Muslim Scientists and Engineers is a group of professionals, para-professionals and near-professionals in science and engineering and related fields, who are also Muslims by faith. AMSE was founded in the late sixties and was later a constitutent organization of the Islamic Society of North America at its founding in the early eighties. AMSE holds its annual conference co-located with the annual convention of ISNA.

North American Islamic Trust (NAIT)

The North American Islamic Trust is a Saudi-backed organization based in Plainfield, Indiana, that owns Islamic properties and promotes Islamic endowments in North America. It is the financial arm of the Muslim Students Association.

NAIT finances and holds titles to mosques, Islamic schools, and other real estate to safeguard and pool the assets of the American Muslim community, develops financial vehicles and financial products that are compatible with both Shari'ah and American law, publishes and distributes Islamic literature, provides legal advice to Muslim organizations, and facilitates and coordinates Islamic community projects.

In 2007, NAIT was named as an unindicted co-conspirator in the Holy Land Foundation terrorist trial, as was board member Jamal Said.

Islamic Centers Division (ICD)

A subsidiary of the North American Islamic Trust, the Islamic Centers Division, which was established in 1981, assists NAIT in the development of mosques, Islamic schools, and Islamic centers throughout the United States. Specifically, ICD manages NAIT's Waqf program, which oversees the funding of such institutions and works to ensure those institutions' permanent designation as Islamic entities. According to the renowned eighth-century Muslim scholar, Imam Abu Hanifa, the term waqf literally means the "detention" of a specific property or object for religious or charitable purposes.

Moreover, ICD protects NAIT's mosques, schools, and Islamic centers against legal actions that may arise. Through its Legal Services Section, ICD provides them with counseling vis a vis such matters as proper transfer of ownership, compliance with zoning regulations, and settlement of previous financial obligations. ICD also assists them with necessities like fund raising, obtaining proper insurance coverage, and securing short-term, interest-free loans.

ICD was included in the 1991 Muslim Brotherhood document as one of the Brotherhood's 29 like-minded "organizations of our friends" that shared the common goal of destroying America and turning it into a Muslim nation. These "friends" were identified by the Brotherhood as groups that could help teach Muslims "that their work in America is a kind of grand Jihad in eliminating and destroying the Western civilization from within and 'sabotaging' its miserable house by their hands so that God's religion [Islam] is made victorious over all others."

American Trust Publications (ATP)

One particularly noteworthy ATP publication is 'Milestones' authored by the late Sayyid Qutb, a pro-jihad leader of the Muslim Brotherhood. In this book, Qutb makes such assertions as:

"Jihad in Islam is simply a name for striving to make this system of life dominant in the world. Wherever an Islamic community exists which is a concrete example of the Divinely ordained system of life, it has a God-given right to step forward and take control of the political authority so that it may establish the Divine system on earth."

"Bringing about the enforcement of the Divine Law (Sharia) and the abolition of man-made laws cannot be achieved only through preaching. When obstacles and practical difficulties are put in its way, it (Islam) has no recourse but to remove them by force."

"Islam has the right to take the initiative. It has the right to destroy all obstacles in the form of institutions and traditions. It is the duty of Islam to annihilate all such systems."

Audio-Visual Center (AVC)

In 1983 AVC set up the largest Muslim-owned commercial audiocassette-duplication facility in the United States. Specializing in Qur'anic albums and other Islamic-related recordings, this facility developed a production capacity of 1.2 million cassettes and CDs per year. AVC also cultivated a large capacity for video recording, production, and graphic arts, as well as an in-house printing facility to meet the needs of ISNA and its affiliates. Many of AVC's books

184

and audio recordings promote Wahhabism, a most extreme form of Islam.

AVC was another organization named in the May 1991 Muslim Brotherhood document as one of the Brotherhood's 29 like-minded "organizations of our friends" that shared the common goal of destroying America and turning it into a Muslim nation. These "friends" were identified by the Brotherhood as groups that could help teach Muslims "that their work in America is a kind of grand Jihad in eliminating and destroying the Western civilization from within and 'sabotaging' its miserable house by their hands so that God's religion, Islam, is made victorious over all other religions."

Muslim Youth of North America (MYNA)

Describing itself as "a self-managed program of the Islamic Society of North America" (ISNA), Muslim Youth of North America is a charitable organization whose constituents and leaders alike are all between the ages of 12 and 18. The group's mission is to "attain the pleasure of Allah" by: "providing a platform for youth expression; fostering an engaging North American Muslim Culture; promoting Islamic principles grounded in Qur'an and Sunnah; sparking youth involvement in community development and dialogue; and establishing a diverse, supportive network of youth in the greater community." Since its inception, MYNA has utilized a variety of strategies designed to spark curiosity about Islam in non-Muslim junior-high and high-school students—e.g., sponsoring soccer teams, offering scholarships, and marketing a line of clothing.

MYNA was the brainchild of ISNA's Youth Committee, which in the summer of 1985 proposed the creation of a continental organization for young Muslims. The ISNA policy-making body endorsed the idea, and as a result MYNA was formally approved and introduced at the First Annual Muslim Youth Winter Conference in December 1985. The initial programs sponsored by MYNA were held at ISNA conferences and conventions.

All of MYNA's financial and operational activities are owned exclusively by ISNA. MYNA's national advisor, Riyad Shamma, is a member of the Majlis Youth Committee that oversees the operations of ISNA's Youth Programming and Services Department. MYNA chairman Omar J. Siddiqui also serves as an ISNA board of directors member. And, according to a report in the Asia Times, MYNA and ISNA have both been closely associated with Tablighi Jamaat, a jihadist organization that serves as a recruiting ground for al Qaeda.

Like ISNA, MYNA is connected in a significant way to the Muslim Brotherhood. Ahmed Elkadi, an Egyptian-born surgeon who headed the U.S. Brotherhood from 1984 to 1994, helped create MYNA in 1985. Moreover, MYNA was also named in the May 1991 Muslim Brotherhood document as one of the Brotherhood's 29 like-minded "organizations of our friends" that shared the common goal of destroying America and turning it into a Muslim nation. Other organizations included in this list, who hold similar charters and purposes, are:

Foundation or International Development (FID)

Islamic Housing Cooperative (IHC)

ISNA FIQH Committee

ISNA Political Awareness Committee (IPAC)

Islamic Education Department (IED)

Muslim Arab Youth Association (MAYA)

Malasian Islamic Study Group (MISG)

Islamic Association For Palestine (IAP)

United Association For Studies and Research (UASR)

Occupied Land Fund (OLF)

Mercy International Association (MIA)

Islamic Circle of North America (ISNA)

Baitul MAL Inc. (BMI)

International Institute For Islamic Thought (IIIT)

Islamic Information Center (IIC)

The 'Investigative Project on Terrorism' discovered this Islamic conspiratorial plan for the silent Islamic Jihad in America. Clearly and explicitly the proposal, and acceptance by most, if not all, of these organizations is to destroy the United States and its religious foundation from within. What is Barack Obama's reaction to their plan and his attitude toward their approach? He embraces them - in his own words.

This is from that interview with Steve Kroft, on 60 Minutes, where Obama made the 'bump in the road' comment after four Americans were murdered in Benghazi, and he refused to blame Islamic radicals. He said:

"Well, I've said even at the time that this is going to be a rocky path. The question presumes that somehow we could have stopped this wave of change. I think it was absolutely the right thing for us to do to align ourselves with democracy, universal rights, a notion that people have to be able to participate in their own governance.

But I was pretty certain and continue to be pretty certain that there are going to be bumps in the road because you know, in a lot of these places the one organizing principle has been Islam, the one part of society that hasn't been controlled completely by the government. There are strains of extremism, and anti-Americanism, and anti-Western sentiment. And you know can be tapped into by demagogues.

There will probably be some times where we bump up against some of these countries and have strong disagreements, but I do think that over the long term, we are more likely to get a Middle East and North Africa that is more peaceful, more prosperous and more aligned with our interests."

Let's repeat for clarity, ("the one organizing principle has been Islam, the one part of society that hasn't been controlled completely by the government.")

Obama's comments fall right in line with that report of the Muslim Brotherhood. To me, it's the 'smoking gun' that links Obama directly to the Muslim Brotherhood intentions. He is sending them millions of our honest American dollars - while he wants more American dollars from more 'rich people.'

Not once in his administration has he criticized either of these organization, their leaders, or the radical Islamists who expressly proclaim from every hilltop in America that they plan to destroy America. He even refuses to acknowledge that Islamic terrorists exist who promise to kill us. From his support of the Islamists, and from his lack of interest in curtailing their plan, one can make only one important conclusion:

Obama clearly supports actions by the Muslim Brotherhood. The Muslim Brotherhood's expressed goal is to "destroy America from within." We must again ask that question: why did he bow to the Saudi king, the leader of Wahabbism, the most radical of Islamism?

This is an article copied from Brietbart that further discloses this plan by the Muslim Brotherhood - supported by

Barack Obama - weakening the United States as we know it:

"In the Spring of this year, US Army Lieutenant Colonel Matthew Dooley was condemned by the Joints Chiefs of Staff (JCS) and relieved of teaching duties at Joint Forces Staff College for teaching a course judged to be offensive to Islam.

The course he taught, 'Perspectives on Islam and Islamic Radicalism', was an elective course that Lt. Col. Dooley's superiors judged as presenting Islam in a negative way. His superiors were persuaded to come to this conclusion after receiving an October, 2011 letter in which 57 Muslim organizations claimed to be offended by the course.

The fact that Lt. Col. Dooley is a highly decorated combat veteran with nearly 20 years of service under his belt apparently held little or no sway with the JCS. As a matter of fact, JCS Chairman General Martin Dempsey personally attacked Lt. Col. Dooley on C-Span on May 10, 2012, during a Pentagon News Conference.

Yet the craziest part of all this is that "the course content, the guest speakers, and the method of instruction" for the course was all approved by the Joint Forces Staff College "years ago."

Former CIA agent Claire M. Lopez commented on the state of things: "All US military Combatant Commands, Services, the National Guard Bureau, and Joint Chiefs are under Dempsey's Muslim Brotherhood-dictated order to ensure that henceforth, no US military course will ever again teach truth about Islam that the jihadist enemy finds offensive (or just too informative)."

Of course this action against Lt. Col. Dooley is outrageous just on the face of it. But one must delve much deeper to understand the grave danger America now faces. The conspiracy is deep and multi-faceted, and is supported even by those who have taken an oath to "protect and defend the United States against all enemies - foreign and domestic."

Of course, Obama's policies created this travesty against Lt. Col. Dooley, but in my mind Obama's character is no better than that. That action can be expected by one of such little character. To me, the real travesty is from the actions by General Dempsey.

I spent over 20 years in the U.S. Air Force, serving a year of that in Saigon, Vietnam. At that time, and ever before and ever since, I have always had a high regard for military officers. They were expected, even of themselves, to be honest and honorable at all times, even under the most dire and self-incriminating situations.

To me, General Dempsey violated that military standard - that code. I realize he was following orders from either the secretary of defense or the president. I absolutely cannot believe he took that action against Lt. Col. Dooley of his own initiative and beliefs. Any honorable military officer would have resigned before committing that unwarranted assault against another military person - especially one of junior rank. That makes General Dempsey just as culpable in supporting the silent American jihad as the president. Who is General Dempsey, anyway? He is an unknown who came out of nowhere - selected, of course, by Barack Obama.

Perhaps that conclusion about Obama and his plans and actions for America must be made and accepted within each individual American heart. That thought is too dire - it's too unbelievable - to be expressed in written words in this insignificant and probably never-to-be-discovered book.

What are the real plans of this man, Barack Obama, who calls himself a Christian, but who too often supports the radical Islamist ideology? Who is this man who prepares for a personal political fund-raising trip to Las Vegas - while he knows four brave and patriotic American citizens are being slaughtered in Benghazi, Libya?

And what about his comment, "I think it was absolutely the right thing for us to do to align ourselves with democracy, universal rights, a notion that people have to be able to participate in their own governance." Has Obama, or more importantly - the women in America who will have all their rights taken away from them - thought about their 'universal rights' when they become assigned to sub-human status? According to the referenced associated comments he made, above, he is planning to align us with the 'peaceful and democratic' Muslim Brotherhood. And, millions of women continue to support him? What is their thinking?

Obama's Ring: The Seat of Satan

Chapter 12

EDUCATION IN AMERICA

On February 8, 2011, CBS News DFW (Dallas/Fort Worth) reportedly ran a story on their website which headlined:

> "Multi-culturalism in America: Texas school district mandates teaching Arabic language and Islam religion in a public school."

The article continued: "Mandatory Arabic Classes Coming To Some Students at Mansfield School District Schools Could Soon Be Learning Arabic As A Required Language.

The school district wants students at select schools to take Arabic language and culture classes as part of a federally funded grant. The Foreign Language Assistance Program (FLAP) grant was awarded to Mansfield ISD last summer by the U.S. Department of Education. As part of the five-year $1.3 million grant, Arabic classes would be mandatory at Cross Timbers Intermediate School and Kenneth Davis Elementary School. The program would also be optional for students at T.A. Howard Middle School and Summit High School. Parents at Cross Timbers say they were caught off-guard by the program and were surprised the district only told them about it in a meeting Monday night between parents and Mansfield ISD Superintendent Bob Morrison.

The DOE has identified Arabic as a 'language of the future.' But parent Joseph Balson was frustrated by the past. "Why are we just now finding out about it?" asked Balson. It's them (Mansfield ISD) applying for the grant, getting it approved and them now saying they'll go back and change it only when they were caught trying to implement this plan without parents knowing about it. Trisha Savage thinks it will offer a well-rounded education."I think its a great opportunity that will open doors. We need to think globally and act locally."

The program was shelved the following day when 200 parents showed up to protest. Many complained that since Christianity could not be taught in schools, Islam should also not be taught in schools. Throughout the nation, however, multi-culturalism, especially Islamic culture, continues to flow into more classrooms.

An article in the San Francisco Chronicle written by Cinnamon Stillwell on June 11, 2008 gave a good long announcement that this Islamic indoctrination was on the way. This action by the Islamists is in accordance with their announced plans that they would do this. Below is that article:

"With fatal terrorist attacks on the decline worldwide

and al Qaeda apparently in disarray, it would seem a time for optimism in the global war on terrorism. But the war has simply shifted to a different arena. Islamists, or those who believe that Islam is a political and religious system that must dominate all others, are focusing less on the military and more on the ideological. It turns out that Western liberal democracies can be subverted without firing a shot.

Nowhere is this more evident than in the educational realm. Islamists have taken what's come to be known as the "soft jihad" into America's classrooms and children in K-12 are the first casualties. Whether it is textbooks, curriculum, classroom exercises, film screenings, speakers or teacher training, public education in America is under assault.

Capitalizing on the post-9/11 demand for Arabic instruction, some public, charter and voucher-funded private schools are inappropriately using taxpayer dollars to implement a religious curriculum. They are also bringing in outside speakers with Islamist ties or sympathies. As a result, not only are children receiving a biased education, but possible violations of the First Amendment's Establishment Clause abound. Consider the following cases:

As reported by the Cabinet Press, a school project last year at Amherst Middle School transformed "the quaint colonial town of Amherst, N.H., into a Saudi Arabian Bedouin tent community." Male and female students were segregated, with the girls hosting "hijab and veil stations" and handing out the oppressive head-to-toe black garment known as the abaya to female guests. Meanwhile, the boys hosted food and Arabic dancing stations because, as explained in the article, "the traditions of Saudi Arabia at this time prevent women from participating in these public roles." An "Islamic religion station" offered up a prayer rug, verses from the Quran, prayer items and a compass pointed towards Mecca. The fact that female subjugation was presented as a benign cultural practice and Islamic religious rituals were promoted with public funds is cause for concern.

Last month, students at Friendswood Junior High in Houston were required to attend an "Islamic Awareness" presentation during class time allotted for physical education. The presentation involved two representatives from the Council on American-Islamic Relations, an organization with a record of Islamist statements and terrorism convictions. According to students, they were taught that "there is one God, his name is Allah" and that "Adam, Noah and Jesus are prophets." Students were also taught about the Five Pillars of Islam and how to pray five times a day and wear Islamic religious garb. Parents were not notified about the presentation and it wasn't until a number of complaints arose that school officials responded with an apologetic e-mail.

Earlier this year at Lake Brantley High School in Seminole County, Fla., speakers from the Academy for Learning Islam gave a presentation to students about "cultural diversity" that extended to a detailed discussion of the Quran and Islam. The school neither screened the ALI speakers nor notified parents. After a number of complaints, local media coverage and a subsequent investigation, the school district apologized for the inappropriate presentation, admitting that it violated the law. Subsequently, ALI was removed from the Seminole County school system's Dividends and Speaker's Bureau.

Tarek ibn Ziyad Academy, a charter school in Inver Grove Heights, Minn., came under recent scrutiny after Minneapolis Star-Tribune columnist Katherine Kersten brought to light concerns about public funding for its overly religious curriculum. The school is housed in the Muslim American Society's (the American Branch of the Egyptian Islamist group the Muslim Brotherhood Minnesota building,) alongside a mosque, and the daily routine includes prayer, ritual washing, halal food preparation and an after-school "Islamic studies" program. Kersten's columns prompted the Minnesota chapter of the American Civil Liberties Union to issue a press release expressing its own reservations about potential First Amendment violations. An investigation initiated by the Minnesota Department of Education verified several of Kersten's allegations and the school has since promised to make the appropriate changes. In a bizarre twist, when a local television news crew tried to report on the findings from school grounds, school officials confronted them and wrestled a camera away from one of its photographers, injuring him in the process.

The controversy surrounding the founding of New York City's Arabic language public school, Khalil Gibran International Academy, last year continues. Former principal Dhabah "Debbie" Almontaser was asked to step down after publicly defending T-shirts produced by Arab Women Active in the Arts and Media, an organization with whom she shared office space, emblazoned with "Intifada NYC." But KGIA has other troublesome associations. Its advisory board includes three imams, one of whom, New York University Imam Khalid Latif, sent a threatening letter to the university's president regarding a planned display of the Danish cartoons. Another, Shamsi Ali, runs the Jamaica Muslim Center Quranic Memorization School in Queens, a replica of the type of Pakistani madrassa (or school) counter-terrorism officials have been warning about since 9/11. Accordingly, several parents founded Stop the Madrassa: A Community Coalition to voice their contention that KGIA is an inappropriate candidate for taxpayer funding.

Equally problematic are the textbooks used in American public schools to teach Islam or Islamic history. Organizations such as Southern California's Council on Islamic Education and Arabic World and Islamic Resources are tasked with screening and editing these textbooks for public school districts, but questions have been raised about the groups' scholarship and ideological agenda. The American Textbook Council, an organization that reviews history and social studies textbooks used in American schools, and its director, Gilbert T. Sewall, have produced a series of articles and reports on Islam textbooks and the findings are damning. They include textbooks that are factually inaccurate, misrepresent and in some cases, glorify Islam, or are hostile to other religions. While teaching students about Islam within a religious studies context may be appropriate, the purpose becomes suspect when the texts involved are compromised in this manner.

Such are the complaints about "History Alive! The Medieval World and Beyond," a textbook published by the Teacher's Curriculum Institute, to the point where parents in the Scottsdale, AZ, school district succeeded in having it removed from the curriculum in 2005. TCI is based in Mountain View, and the textbook is now being used in the state's public schools, where similar concerns have arisen. A Marin County mother whose son has been assigned "History Alive!" has been trying to mount an effort to call school officials' attention to the problem. Similarly, a San Luis Obispo mother filed an official complaint several years ago with her son's school authorities over the use of Houghton Mifflin's middle school text, "Across the Centuries," which has been widely criticized for whitewashing Islamic history and glorifying Islam. Its inclusion in the Montgomery County, Md. public school curriculum among other districts across the country, could lead to further objections.

But the forces in opposition are powerful and plenty. They include public education bureaucrats and teachers mired in naivete and political correctness, biased textbook publishers, politicized professors and other experts tasked with helping states approve textbooks, and at the top of the heap, billions of dollars in Saudi funding. These funds are pouring into the coffers of various organizations that design K-12 curricula. The resultant material, not coincidentally, turns out to be inaccurate, biased and, considering the Wahhabist strain of Islam promulgated by Saudi Arabia, dangerous. And again, taxpayer dollars are involved. National Review Online contributing editor Stanley Kurtz explains:

"The United States government gives money — and a federal seal of approval — to a university Middle East Studies center. That center offers a government-approved K-12 Middle East studies curriculum to America's teachers. But in fact, that curriculum has been bought and paid for by the Saudis, who may even have trained the personnel who operate the university's outreach program. Meanwhile, the American government is asleep at the wheel — paying scant attention to how its federally mandated public outreach programs actually work. So without ever realizing it, America's taxpayers end up subsidizing — and providing official federal approval for — K-12 educational materials on the Middle East that have been created under Saudi auspices. Game, set, match: Saudis."

Along with funding textbooks and curricula, the Saudis are also involved in funding and designing training for public school teachers. The Saudi funded Prince Alwaleed Bin Talal Center for Muslim-Christian Understanding at Georgetown University now offers professional development workshops for K-12 teachers. The workshops take place at the hosting institution and provide teachers with classroom material. They are free of charge and ACMCU throws in lunch to boot.

But this generosity likely comes with a catch, for the center is known for producing scholars and material with a decidedly apologist bent, both toward the Saudi royal family and Islamic radicalism. It's no accident that ACMCU education consultant Susan Douglass, according to her bio, has been "an affiliated scholar" with the Council on Islamic Education "for over a decade." Douglass also taught social studies at the Islamic Saudi Academy in Fairfax, Va., where her husband still teaches. ISA has come under investigation for Saudi-provided textbooks and curriculum that some have alleged promotes hatred and intolerance towards non-

Muslims. That someone with Douglass' problematic associations would be in charge of training public school teachers hardly inspires confidence in the system.

While groups such as People for the American Way, Americans United for Separation of Church and State, and the ACLU express outrage at any semblance of Christianity in America's public schools, very little clamor has met the emergence of Islam in the same arena. An occasional press release, such as the one put out by the Minnesota chapter of the ACLU regarding TIZA, will surface, but by and large, the arbiters of separation of church and state or in this case, mosque and state, have gone silent. The same can largely be said for the federal government and, in particular, the State Department. No doubt, Saudi dollars and influence are part of the problem.

Probably the single greatest weapon in the arsenal of those trying to fight the misuse of America's public schools is community involvement. As noted previously, a number of parental coalitions have sprung up across the country in an effort to protect their own children from indoctrination. The Stop the Madrassa Coalition has expanded its efforts beyond New York City by working on policy ideas for legislation and meeting privately with members of Congress. Also providing hope are Rep. Sue Myrick (R-N.C.), whose 10-point "Wake Up America" agenda includes a call to reform Saudi-provided textbooks, and the bipartisan Congressional Anti-Terrorism Caucus she co-chairs. Its focus on "jihadist ideology" demonstrates an all-too-rare governmental understanding of the nature of the current conflict.

The power to educate the next generation is an inestimable one and a free society cedes control at its peril. The days of the "silent majority" are no longer tenable in the face of a determined and clever enemy. The battle of ideas must be joined." End of article.

With our government, at all levels, abetting, allowing, and supporting this creeping danger to change our great country into values, Islamic or Socialistic, foreign to our birthright and history, what actions can we take to stop it? The two articles above give good clues that concerned communities must take direct action. If those insidious actions can't be changed however, then individual families and their children must make that change back to patriotism individually and as a family.

This is another article, published by Aaron Klein, January 23, 2013, that shows the insidious attack on our education system - and America, by the Islamists. Aaron Klein is WND's (WorldNetDaily) senior staff reporter and Jerusalem bureau chief. He also hosts 'Aaron Klein Investigative Radio' on New York's WABC Radio.

The article begins: "A Muslim Brotherhood-linked organization has partnered with the U.S. Department of Education and the State Department to facilitate an online program aiming to connect all U.S. schools with classrooms abroad by 2016." Vartan Gregorian, a board member of the organization, the Qatar Foundation International, was appointed in 2009 to President Obama's White House Fellowships Commission. WND previously exposed that Gregorian served as a point man in granting $49.2 million in startup capital to an education-reform project founded by former Weather Underground terrorist William Ayers and chaired by Obama.

Documentation shows Gregorian was central in Ayers' recruitment of Obama to serve as the first chairman of the project, the Chicago Annenberg Challenge – a job in which Obama worked closely on a regular basis with Ayers. Obama also later said his job at the project qualified him to run for public office, as WND previously reported.

Connecting schools to fulfill Obama pledge

The Qatar Foundation International, or QFI, in 2011 partnered with the Department of State and the U.S.

Department of Education to facilitate matchmaking between classrooms in the U.S. and international schools through something called the "Connect All Schools" project. QFI, funded by the Qatari government, explains on its website the initiative was founded in response to Obama's call in his June 2009 speech to the Arab world in Cairo, Egypt, to "create a new online network, so a young person in Kansas can communicate instantly with a young person in Cairo."

QFI relates how more than 100 U.S. schools and organizations have already connected on the interactive website. The stated goal of the initiative is to "connect every school in the U.S. with the world by 2016." This is not the QFI's first foray into the U.S. education system. WND reported last may the Qatar-based foundation awarded "Curriculum Grants" to seven U.S. schools and language organizations to "develop comprehensive and innovative curricula and teaching materials to be used in any Arabic language classroom."

QFI, based in Washington, D.C., is the U.S. branch of the Qatar Foundation, founded in 1995 by Qatar's ruling emir, Sheikh Hamad bin Khalifa Al Thani. Thani is still the group's vice-chairman, while one of his three wives, Sheikha Moza bint Nasser, chairs the organization's board. Thani also launched Al Jazeera in 1996 and served as the television network's chairman. The Qatar foundation is close to the Muslim Brotherhood.

In January 2012, it launched the Research Center for Islamic Legislation and Ethics under the guidance of Tariq Ramadan, who serves as the center's director. Ramadan is the grandson of the notorious founder of the Muslim Brotherhood, Hassan al Banna. Ramadan was banned from the U.S. until 2010 when the Obama administration issued him a visa to give a lecture at a New York school.

QFI, meanwhile, named several institutions after Yusuf al-Qaradawi, one of the top leaders of the Muslim Brotherhood. Many regard Qaradawi as the de facto spiritual leader of Egypt's Muslim Brotherhood. The foundation instituted the Sheikh Yusuf Al Qaradawi Scholarships and in 2009 established a research center named the Qaradawi Center for Islamic Moderation and Renewal.

Qaradawi has personally attended scores of foundation events, including conferences at which he served as a keynote speaker.Qaradawi achieved star status because of his regular sermons and interviews on Al Jazeera. The Investigative Project on Terrorism documents Qardawi openly permitted the killing of American troops in Iraq and praised the "heroic deeds" of "Hamas, Jihad, Al-Aqsa Brigades and others."

Obama, Ayers Connection

Gregorian, president of Carnegie Corp. charitable foundation, was appointed by Obama in 2009 as a White House fellow. Born in Tabriz, Iran, Gregorian served for eight years as president of the New York Public Library and was also president of Brown University. As Brown president, Gregorian served on the selection committee of the Annenberg Foundation, which funded Ayers' Chicago Annenberg Challenge with a $49.2 million, 2-to-1 matching challenge grant over five years. Ayers was one of five founding members of the Annenberg Challenge who wrote to the Annenberg Foundation for the initial funding.

Steve Diamond, a political-science and law professor and a blogger who has posted on Obama, previously posted a letter from Nov. 18, 1994, in which Gregorian, serving as the point man on Annenberg's selection committee, asked Ayers to "compose the governing board" of the Challenge's collaborative project with "people who reflect the racial and ethnic diversity of Chicago."

Ayers and other founding Challenge members then recruited Obama to serve as the project chairman. WND was first to expose that Obama and Ayers used the project grant

203

money to fund organizations run by radicals tied to Ayers, including Mike Klonsky, a former top communist activist who was a senior leader in the Students for a Democratic Society group, a major leftist student organization in the 1960s from which the Weathermen terror group later splintered. National Review Online writer Stanley Kurtz examined the project archives housed at the Richard J. Daley Library at the University of Illinois at Chicago, finding Obama and Ayers worked closely at the project. The documents obtained by Kurtz showed Ayers served as an ex-officio member of the board that Obama chaired through the project's first year. Ayers also served on the board's governance committee with Obama and worked with him to craft project bylaws, according to the documents.

Ayers made presentations to board meetings chaired by Obama. Ayers also spoke for the Chicago School Reform Collaborative before Obama's board, while Obama periodically spoke for the board at meetings of the collaborative, the project documents reviewed by Kurtz show. WND reported Obama and Ayers also served together on the board of the Woods Fund, a liberal Chicago nonprofit that granted money to far-left causes. One of the groups funded by the Woods Fund was the Midwest Academy, an activist organization modeled after Marxist community organizer Saul Alinsky described as teaching tactics of direct action, confrontation and intimidation.

WND reported Jackie Kendall, executive director of the Midwest Academy, was on the team that developed and delivered the first Camp Obama training for volunteers aiding Obama's campaign through the 2008 Iowa Caucuses. Camp Obama was a two to four-day intensive course run in conjunction with Obama's campaign aimed at training volunteers to become activists to help Obama win the presidential election.

Obama scholar linked to 'Ground Zero' imam

Meanwhile, WND reported Gregorian is closely tied to the Muslim leaders behind the controversial Islamic cultural center to be built near the site of the Sept. 11 attacks. Gregorian also serves on the board of the Sept. 11 Memorial and Museum. The museum is reportedly working with the American Society for Muslim Advancement, whose leaders are behind the mosque, to ensure the future museum will represent the voices of American Muslims.

"The Sept. 11 museum will represent the voices of American Muslims in particular, and it will honor members of other communities who came together in support and collaboration with the Muslim community on September 11 and its aftermath," stated Daisy Khan, executive director of the society. The Sept. 11 museum's oral historian, Jenny Pachucki, is collaborating with the society to ensure the perspective of American Muslims is woven into the overall experience of the museum, according to the museum's blog. Khan's husband, Feisal Abdul Rauf, is the founder of the society as well as chairman of Cordoba Initiative, which is behind the proposed mosque to be built about two blocks from the area referred to as Ground Zero.

With Gregorian at its helm, Carnegie Corp. is at the top of the list of society supporters on the Islamic group's website. Carnegie is also listed as a funder of both of the society's partner organizations, Search for Common Ground and the United Nations Alliance of Civilizations. Gregorian was a participant in the U.N. body's first forum, as was Rauf. Rauf is vice chairman on the board of the Interfaith Center of New York, which honored Gregorian at an awards dinner in 2008.

World domination

Gregorian is the author of "Islam: A Mosaic, Not A Monolith." According to a book review by the Middle East Forum, his book "establishes the Islamist goal of world

205

domination." A chapter of the book, "Islamism: Liberation Politics," quotes Ayatollah Khomeini: "Islam does not conquer. Islam wants all countries to become Muslim, of themselves." Hassan al-Banna, founder of the Muslim Brotherhood, is quoted stating it "is the nature of Islam to dominate, not to be dominated, to impose its laws on all nations and to extend its power to the entire planet." Gregorian himself recommends for Muslims a system he calls "theo-democracy," which he defines as "a divine democratic government" that, according to the book review, "would have a limited popular sovereignty under the suzerainty of Allah." End of article.

The following extract from my book, 'American Heroes: Students Who Learn' is inserted here to help with that individual family process. It's written directly to those young people who will carry our American heritage forward, hopefully the way our Founding Fathers planned. It's offered as a direct counter to the indoctrination and Islamic brainwashing Obama and his Muslim Brotherhood associates have already begun.

A MESSAGE TO PATRIOTIC AMERICAN STUDENTS

Okay, so you are a student in the fifth, sixth, seventh, or eighth grade and you wonder why school and learning stuff is so necessary. Everybody tells you it's so important, but you already know how to read, write, and count. You probably ask why you should keep studying so hard trying to learn more when you already know how to read and count. Maybe that's true. Maybe if you can just read and count you can get by in society. Maybe you can find a job that pays someone who can just read and count. That job might be enough to let you survive and get by, or it might be enough if you always have to ask your parents or other relatives to help;

to give you money when you need it to pay rent and buy food. Maybe you can just survive by just reading and counting, but is that enough to make you happy? Is that enough to be able to help your friends when they need help?

Being able to read and count is very important. Long ago it was even enough to get a good job if you knew someone who would let you try that job to prove how effective you were. Now there are so many people who can read and count and do so much more that most good jobs are reserved for them. An employer always asks, "Why should I hire someone who can barely read and count when I have so many other more qualified workers to choose from? Why should I waste my time on someone less qualified?"

But, trying to learn more, and do your best, is more than just for getting a good job and having enough money to buy things you need and want. We all look forward to those things as students and even as adults. It's great to have a nice car, a pretty house, and many good friends. Now, in this current society, having a good education - learning - is becoming even more important. It's not just for helping you get things. Now, it's for helping you understand more complex and important things to protect your country. Without your country, the United States of America, being preserved in the way our original Founders intended, your children and grandchildren might never feel the freedoms under which you live, today.

One of the great founders of our country was Thomas Jefferson. Jefferson, along with others who developed our Constitution, the document designed to guide the way we have freedom and liberty in America without infringing upon other's freedom and liberty, was greatly concerned about our education system of the future. His strong proposal was that education should be guided by the principle of teaching citizens, children, how to protect themselves against individuals or groups who would use their elected positions to destroy the principles of our Constitution which guarantee freedom and free will to every American citizen. Never has our country, the America we love, been in such jeopardy that Thomas Jefferson warned us about.

As a learning student, you are now the most important citizen to help preserve the principles of our Constitution that protect our American freedom. Now, it's not enough that you just learn how to read and count. Now, you must learn to read, interpret, and understand every word and subtle meaning of our Constitution. Our Constitution and way of life as free citizens are being attacked. This attack is very sneaky and subtle. There are no bombs being dropped; there are no fire alarms ringing; and there is no one yelling, 'fire.' Our attackers are very sneaky. Their plans don't match their words. They don't yell, "charge," that they are attacking.

Those who plan to change our way of life without our approval say nice words that sound really great. They say what we are going to do for more people. They say how we will all be more equal, and how all our work will be more evenly shared. They say they will spread our wealth around to other people. They suggest that those who have more things we all hope to get, like more money, nice cars, and bigger houses, are greedy and selfish and don't care about their fellow citizens. They say nothing about those people having to educate themselves and work to earn those things.

To someone who can only read and count and have not tried to be successful, these things sound really great. It means they can have more success, all the nice things they want, without having to learn more and work hard. They can be successful by learning and working, or by just being lazy and letting our government give them more things most people work so hard to get.

This is the danger and treachery Thomas Jefferson warned us about if education just focuses on reading and counting. Education must also include enough knowledge to defend ourselves against tyranny and treachery. That knowledge means you must understand the underlying and hidden meaning of each word and phrase. People can use nice words and flowery words to make you believe they are

208

trying to do good things for you. It's only a sneaky way to make you support them, and vote for their ideas. They will promise you anything to make you vote for them, to give them more power.

Conflict of Values

Even though our ancestors worked together to write our Constitution which now protects our freedom, they had many differing opinions during that process. They looked at the same questions and saw many different answers. Some thought it would be better to have a strong central government to make sure citizens of all the states were treated equally. They thought more control would make better democracy.

Others, including Thomas Jefferson, saw a great danger if the central government had too much power. How could citizens defend their freedoms if one central power was in control of everything? What if the leader of that central power was more focused on his own position of power than on allowing more citizens to have their individual power of self determination? What if that central leader with that much power decided to make his child the next leader of America without having elections and votes? Who could stop him?

This difference of opinion regarding a question, how to write the Constitution, is controlled by a conflict of values. Some want others to be allowed to decide their own freedom and destiny; others want to be in a position of power to give it to them. If all leaders were honorable, this would not create the problem Thomas Jefferson anticipated. Everyone could still enjoy liberty and freedom - so long as the leader allows it. The problem is that too much power corrupts the leader. That leader sees and evaluates things only from his or her one view. That view often conflicts with other people's views and needs. Eventually, that leader becomes a tyrant. Even a good tyrant restricts the free will of citizens.

When one group, one organization, or one person tries to control the actions and desires of others, that is not the way our Constitution was conceived and written. We each must be allowed to succeed in our own individual way. Others must not determine that route for us, and others should not be in a position to force us to support their success. For example, we should be allowed to go directly to an employer to ask for a job we want. We should not be required to join or ask another control group before we are allowed to ask for that job - to seek that personal success.

Many people with honorable intentions to be good workers for themselves and their employers are not allowed to do that because their future is controlled by another organization that determines their destiny.

To be able to see that burdensome handicap, you must be able to do more than read, write, and count. You must learn, and have enough insight and understanding to comprehend how things are merged. In other words, if others are controlling your destiny, you will never have the right success path that will allow you to reach your highest level of happiness. In a group that controls your success, the only one who will be rewarded is the one fulfilling his goals of power and control. You will only be a controlled puppet. The leader of that group just wants more power to control you, and any others he can.

Socialism and Capitalism

To be a hero and to be someone who tries to learn more than reading, writing, and counting, there are two concepts that are very important to understand. These are the concepts of socialism and capitalism.

Our country, The United States of America, and our Constitution, were based on the concept of capitalism. This is also called the 'free enterprise' system. This is based on the idea that each person in the United States is free to decide what job or profession he or she would like to do, and how far they would like to succeed. It means that they can choose to get an education, get a job of their choice, or start a business of their own. They don't have to ask anyone's permission to make that choice, as long as that activity is legal. Capitalism is a free choice system.

Socialism is completely different. Under socialism, the government controls almost everything. Under extreme socialistic conditions, the government tells you if you can go to school, which school you will go to, if you can go to college, and what job you can have. The government assigns you to a job. Then the money you make is shared with all other workers under that system. If you are lazy and don't like to work, you still get the same pay as anyone who works hard and tries to do his or her best.

Under this system, everybody is treated the same, except for those in charge. They decide what they want and need, and they decide what you need and can have. Ordinarily, those in charge always stay in charge because they never let anyone else have that power position. Socialism means workers have no determination about how much success they will have.

Would you like to work harder than everyone else, then get the same as the others who do nothing? If you decide to do only what the others do, do you think your workplace can be successful? If all workplaces are like that, can your country, America, be successful and allow anyone else to be successful?

These are the basic differences between capitalism and socialism. Socialism is not guided or allowed by our Constitution. Your choice to be a hero will be determined by your respect for our Constitution, your love of your family and friends, and your idea to make America a better place for your children. You must now be a new American hero to protect that Constitution that protects you, your future, your happiness, and our country - our America.

Duty

Who do we usually think of when words such as: duty, honor, country, sacrifice, and dedication are used? It's common to think of people who are in the armed services, military people, since they are on the front lines often exposing their lives to bullets and bombs from dangerous enemies. Once they take an oath to defend our country, they are honor- bound to perform that duty.

Other Americans, merely by the act of not rejecting their American citizenship, are also honor-bound and historically obligated to fulfill that duty. That unspoken oath comes with their acceptance of citizenship. Of course their duty is different, since they don't bear military arms to defend America. Their duty is to contribute something to make America even better and to choose leaders who will be the best to defend America and our Constitution. To do that, they must be educated enough to get a job and to understand when politicians make false promises, or promises to do something that shows disrespect to our Constitution.

As a student, your duty is to help protect our country and make America even better. You will be a real American hero when you study and learn enough to read and write well, understand numbers, and interpret the dangers that threaten America.

Once you understand those dangers, as an American hero you will be able to make the right choices. Those right choices will allow America to still be the great land of opportunity when your children step forward to be more heroes to defend America. Those dangers will not go away. They will always be trying to destroy our freedom. There will always be someone who becomes a leader of America who will not fully support our Constitution. You must be prepared, by learning enough, to recognize them.

Thomas Jefferson will be proud of you when you are able to do this. Other loyal Americans will also respect you and be proud of you when you do your best to become a good citizen and a proud and loyal American.

In a recent entry on my blog site at Authorsden, and in a letter to the editor of a state-wide newspaper, I emphasized that the U.S. Department of Education should be eliminated because it was ineffective, complicated the education process, and does not allow or encourage effective or reasonable education. Now, I've changed my mind. The U.S. Department of Education should be eliminated, destroyed, and totally obliterated; not because it's simply ineffective, but because it's a danger to our national safety and security. Our education bureaucracy at many levels is ignoring education essentials to develop a successful person. Now, they are focused only on social and cultural aspects. They want a compliant person in accordance with the prevailing plan; whether that be Socialistic principles or Islamic dogma.

Even the top person in the education chain, Arne Duncan, recently discredited himself, his country, and our children. One would expect the education leader, the education secretary at the federal level would set an example of honesty to give his department unquestioned credibility. He dishonored that essential standard when he recently lied about results of the 2013 sequestration.

He claimed many teachers had already been fired, given their 'pink slips' because of the sequestration. In fact, no teachers had got their pink slips at that time for that reason. How can students believe in the system in which they must adhere if they know the leader of that system does not tell the truth? If they can't trust him, how can they trust the system that provides their future?

I repeat; we do not need a national education system. It detracts from educational results rather than supports it. Our education focus must be on our children - not on a system.

Obama's Ring: The Seat of Satan

Chapter 13

THE MUSLIM BROTHERHOOD

Perhaps this chapter should be numbered: Chapter 666 equals 18. In an earlier part of this book, I explained the significance and the relationship of the number 666 and its quantitative value of 18. There are many other interesting relationships found in number associations in the Bible. One is the relevance of '666 is 18' and how that perfectly matches the number of letters in the BARACKHUSSEINOBAMA name.

Another important relationship number that popped into my thoughts as I typed 'the end' to this book was the number 13. I had planned only 12 chapters. I couldn't imagine why the number 13 was so important to this message, and why I couldn't get the feeling of fulfillment at the end of Chapter 12.

We are all aware of the imaginary or perceived significance of the number 13. It's considered a bad omen - a number to be avoided. Certainly one would not want to be number 13 in a list of people. The number 13 is so significant that some tall buildings do not even have a floor identified with the number 13. The number 13 is the 'bad luck number.' So, why did that number haunt me so devilishly when I thought I had finished this book. Finally, I remembered.

The Bible Book of Revelation is the most dynamic and detailed book in the Bible. It's very specific. Reading closer, one finds that Chapter 13 in the Book of Revelation is the most specific. I had not realized until now that it's the Chapter I referenced most in this book. It's important beyond imagination. It's so important that John wrote in Verse 9, "If any man have an ear, let him hear." John began Verse 18 with, "Here is wisdom. Let him that hath understanding count the number of the beast."

This is also the chapter that clearly introduces the 'seven heads' the 'second beast' and the 'number of the first beast.' It's all there in the short Chapter 13. If you haven't read this chapter in the Book of Revelation, I encourage you to do so, now, before you finish reading this chapter in this book. It's that important - and when you are to this point in this book, that chapter becomes very understandable. Some of those things revealed in Chapter 13 could only be interpreted in these modern times.

During my research for this book project I discovered that the Book of Daniel has some references very similar to those in the Book of Revelation. Perhaps the most important and currently relevant verse that describes events of today is Daniel 11:39, referencing the beast:

> "Thus shall he do in the most strong holds with a strange god, whom he shall acknowledge and increase with glory; and he shall cause them to rule over many, and shall divide the land for gain."

Currently, there's a strong movement in the United States and the entire Western World to replace our God with a strange god. It's a god discovered or created by others 600 years after Jesus was crucified. It's a god that did not exist when Daniel wrote his Book, so perhaps that's why Daniel saw him as a 'strange' god. Also, that strange god seems to demand obedience and subservience, often through force and conquest if necessary. Our God offers salvation through acceptance and belief.

To Christians, that other god is indeed a 'strange' god. Even the information about that god is strange and confusing. It has many sources and interpretations, often at the whim of a local imam. That god was 'strange' to the writers of our Bible - because he did not exist at the time the Bible was written. How could they have given him a name, other than 'strange?'

Basically, the followers of that god have two references that guide them. The Koran and the Hadith. The Koran is often spelled different ways which also creates some confusion: Koran, Quran, and Qu'ran. An understanding of the definition of these two will help with the following discussion.

The Koran, their 'Holy Koran,' is the sacred writings of Islam revealed by God to the prophet Muhammad during his life at Mecca and Medina. This is the document most referenced.

The Hadith, according to Merriam-Webster, is a narrative record of the sayings or customs of Muhammad and his companions. Many of the harsher and more violent ideas are from the Hadith. This allows critics of Islam to be disarmed when Muslims respond, "Those things are not in the Koran." These two references are used in the following discussions about Islam, the Muslim Brotherhood, Wahhabism, and the silent and secret attack on America from within.

Let's begin by trying to understand the concept of Wahhabism and how it's trying to destroy us - and who the major players are. In an earlier chapter I explained the ideological differences between the two major divisions of

Islam: the Shia and the Sunni. The Shia believe their Mahdi (their Messiah) is already on earth waiting to be activated. An example I gave was Iran trying to create such havoc that he must expose himself to make the world 'pure." The Sunni believe the Mahdi has not yet returned. So, how does Wahhabism fit into this confusion?

Wahhabism is an ultra-conservative branch of Sunni Islam. It's a religious movement among fundamentalist Islamic believers, with an aspiration to return to the earliest fundamental Islamic sources of the Quran and Hadith, with inspiration from the teachings of Medieval theologian Ibn Taymiyyah and early jurist Ahmad ibn Hanbal. Wahhabism was a popular revivalist movement instigated by an eighteenth century theologian, Muhammad ibn Abd al-Wahhab (1703–1792) from Najd, Saudi Arabia.

He began his movement through peaceful discussions with attendees of various shrines and eventually gained popular support by convincing the local Amir, Uthman ibn Mu'ammar, to help him in his struggle. His has become the dominant form of Islam in Saudi Arabia. The movement claims to adhere to the correct understanding of the general Islamic doctrine of Tawid, on the "uniqueness" and "unity" of God, shared by the majority of Islamic sects, but with an emphasis on advocating following of the Athari school of thought only.

Ibn Abd-al-Wahhab was influenced by the writings of Ibn Taymiyya and questioned the prevalent philosophical interpretations of Islam being the Ash'ari and Maturidi schools, claiming to rely on the Qur'an and the Hadith without speculative philosophy so as to not transgress beyond the limits of the early Muslims known as the Salaf. He attacked a "perceived moral decline and political weakness" in the Arabian Peninsula and condemned what he perceived as idolatry, the popular cult of saints, and shrine and tomb visitation.

The terms Wahhabi and Salafi and ahl al-hadith

218

(people of hadith) are often used interchangeably, but Wahhabism has also been called "a particular orientation within Salafism", and an orientation considered ultra-conservative and apolitical. Salafism, on the other hand, has been termed as the hybridation between the teachings of Ibn Abdul-Wahhab and others which have taken place since the 1960s.

The movement gained unchallenged precedence in the Arabian Peninsula through an alliance between Muhammad ibn Abd al-Wahhab and the House of Muhammad ibn Saud who provided political and financial power for the religious revival represented by Ibn Abd al-Wahhab. The writer El Khabar Ousbouî suggests the popularity of the Wahhabi movement is in part due to this alliance and the funding of several religious channels.

The House of Saud still owns Saudi Arabia and still actively promotes Wahhabism. With all their wealth from oil revenues their influence is found in every sector of American society, especially education, to fulfill the Wahhabi Islamic fundamentalist mission of making Islam the only religion in the world. Although they silently and surreptitiously function with influence and petro-dollars, their hate for the Western World is exposed when most of the September 2011 attackers on the World Trade Center were Saudis. Do the Saudis function under strict Islamic ideology, or are they now more worldly and considerate to their 'fellow man?'

Beheading is mentioned in our Bible regarding the 'beast' and those who support him. What is Saudi Arabia's thought on beheading? And, what does that have to do with America as we exist, today? It should be a complicated answer, but it's not when the full details and connections are exposed. Let's begin with how casual the Saudi's are about beheading.

The following information is from an article by Ryan Villareal in the International Business Times, dated September 11, 2012. The article is titled, 'Justice by the

Sword: Saudi Arabia's Embrace of the Death Penalty.'

"Four people were executed by beheading in Saudi Arabia Tuesday, bringing the total number of executions to 57 so far this year, according to the AFP News Agency. Three were Saudi citizens and one a Palestinian. The four men were found guilty in three separate cases and executed in three different cities.

Two Saudi men, Mohammed bin Ahmed Kharmi and Musa bin Mohsen Kharmi, were convicted of armed robbery and beheaded in the city of Jizan. A Palestinian, Wael Anba, had stabbed a Yemeni man to death and was executed in Jeddah. The third Saudi man, Saad al-Mansuri, was beheaded in Buraida for shooting a fellow citizen to death with a machine gun.

The number of executions in Saudi Arabia nearly tripled from 27 in 2010 to 79 in 2011 and the Persian Gulf state remains one of 21 nations known currently to carry out the death penalty, according to Amnesty International. "In Saudi Arabia death sentences were mostly handed down after court proceedings that failed to satisfy international standards of fair trial," Amnesty said in a 2011 report. "Foreign nationals, particularly migrant workers from developing countries in Africa and Asia, were sentenced to death and remained particularly vulnerable to the secretive and summary nature of the criminal justice process."

In June 2011, an Indonesian woman working as a housemaid, Ruyati Binti Sapubi, was executed after she butchered her Saudi employer with a meat cleaver, citing persistent abuse and being refused leave to return home to see her family. Indonesia placed a moratorium on sending domestic workers to Saudi Arabia, following Sapubi's execution."

Iqbal Athes (CNN) Jan 25, 2013

"Sri Lanka will limit the amount of women that go to Saudi Arabia to work as housemaids as outrage continues over Saudi Arabia's beheading of a Sri Lankan teen. Officials this week raised the minimum age for female domestic workers so that no women under the age of 25 would be allowed to go to Saudi Arabia to work as a maid," said Keheliya Rambukwella, a government spokesman.

The move comes after the beheading of housemaid Rizana Nafeek that occurred earlier this month. Nafeek was 17 when a baby she was caring for in Saudi Arabia died. She was convicted of killing her employers' son in 2005. The family said she strangled the 4-month-old boy after being asked to bottle-feed him, but Nafeek said the infant accidentally choked on milk."

Seven beheaded for stealing

(CNN) -- Seven men were executed by beheading Wednesday in Saudi Arabia for stealing, according to SPA, the official Saudi New agency.

The deaths came a day after the United Nations called for the kingdom not to carry out the punishment, in part because the men had allegedly not been given fair trials. The U.N. said the men were reportedly accused of organizing a criminal group, armed robbery, raiding and breaking into jewelry stores in 2005. (They were juveniles when arrested.)

The U.N. special rapporteur on torture, Juan E. Mendez, said there are also grave concerns that the men were tortured during detention and forced to sign confessions.

"This is not the only breach in Saudi Arabia's international obligations under international law, which imposes an outright prohibition on torture, it is also in breach of the government's international obligation under the

Convention against Torture that explicitly forbids the use of all forms of torture for the purpose of extracting confessions or acquiring information," he said.

SPA issued a statement on behalf of the Ministry of Interior that starts with a Quranic verse from the chapter 'The Table Spread.'

"The punishment of those who wage war against God and His Messenger, and strive with might and main for mischief through the land is: execution, or crucifixion, or the cutting off of hands and feet from opposite sides, or exile from the land: that is their disgrace in this world, and a heavy punishment is theirs in the Hereafter."

Saudi Arabia, one of the few remaining absolute monarchies in the world, has a criminal justice system that is based on a strict interpretation of sharia law as set forth in the Islamic holy book, the Quran. The death penalty is typically handed down for violent crimes, including murder, rape, and armed robbery, but also for drug trafficking, adultery, sodomy, apostasy (renunciation of religion, meaning Islam), and "sorcery."

Beheading is the preferred method of execution in Saudi Arabia, though it was not applied to women until the 1990s. Other methods include death by firing squad and public stoning in cases of adultery. Human rights groups have criticized the Saudi criminal justice system over its lack of transparency and due process, as well as for applying the death penalty to those who were minors at the time they committed their crimes, a practice prohibited by international law under the U.N. Convention on the rights of the Child. "Countries around the world have banned this barbaric punishment for children," said Jo Becker, children's rights advocacy director at Human Rights Watch, in a 2010 statement. "Saudi Arabia should seize the opportunity to end this practice around the world once and for all."

Saudi Arabia's prominence as one of the world's major exporters of oil and a key ally of the U.S. in the region, however, has largely insulated it from serious criticism by major foreign powers that might be able to pressure the kingdom to improve its record on human rights."

In Saudi Arabia, the heads of the executed are sewn back on by a doctor immediately after they have been severed by a swift stroke of a scimitar, if done properly. Afterward, the bodies are transported to be buried in unmarked graves. An Arabian scimitar figures prominently on the flag of Saudi Arabia.

At the moment Saudi Arabia is considering abandoning beheading as a death penalty. But, it's not for the reason one would think. It's because they are running short of those most skilled in beheading. They are considering using firing squads instead.

Saudi Arabia is not the only Muslim country that considers the use of beheading. Those tragedies abound and are used even by common Islamists for grudges and retribution. The following is from a report in the Daily Record.com.uk, on March 13, 2013, about an incident on November 30, 2012:

"A 14-year-old Afghan girl was beheaded and killed in an attack by two men, one of whom apparently asked her to marry him. The attack happened Tuesday, a day before new legislation was introduced in Congress calling on the U.S. government to take steps to help protect Afghan women and girls as the U.S. military prepares to exit Afghanistan.

Gasitina, a student, was beheaded in the Imam Sahib district of the Kunduz province. The attack was initially reported by local media, and was confirmed by Amnesty International researcher, Horia Mosadiq, in an email.

The girl was fetching water when she was accosted, according to reports. The men, who have not been identified, were arrested by police. The girl and her parents had refused a marriage proposal by one of the men, according to the Amnesty International report.

223

This was the 15th deadly attack on a female victim in Kunduz in 2012, the human rights organization said. "Amnesty International is very concerned about the violations against women in Afghanistan," said Cristina Finch, director of the organizations's Women's Human Rights program."

This review of Saudi Arabia's policies, interpretations and actions according to their beliefs must make us take a hard, serious look at their Wahhabist plans for the United States. We, our government and individually, have not.

We as individuals have assumed our government would protect us from such insidious jeopardy. We have been deadly wrong - many in our government, even at the highest level, seem involved in that silent encroachment against our country and our freedom. While our government removes major obstacles to that attack, the attack continues - especially in our schools. This is part of a report from a study conducted by 'Freedom House.' highlighting that danger.

Wahhabism in the United States

'Wahhabism in the United States:' A study conducted by the non-governmental organization, 'Freedom House' found Wahhabi publications in a Mosque in the United States. These publications included statements that Muslims should not only "always oppose infidels "in every way, but "hate them for their religion for Allah's sake", that "democracy" is responsible for all the horrible wars of the 20th century", and that "Shia Islam" and certain Sunni Muslims were "apostasy in Islam."

The Saudi government issued a response to this report, stating: "It has worked diligently during the last five years to overhaul its education system but overhauling an educational system is a massive undertaking."

A review of the study by 'Institute for Social Policy and

Understanding' complained the study cited documents from only a few mosques, arguing most mosques in the U.S. are not under Wahhabi influence. Freedom House comments on the study were not entirely negative however, and concluded: American-Muslim leaders must thoroughly scrutinize this study.

Despite its limitations, the study highlights an ugly undercurrent in modern Islamic discourse that American-Muslims must openly confront. However, in the vigor to expose strains of extremism, we must not forget that open discussion is the best tool to debunk the extremist literature rather than a suppression of "First Amendment to the United States Constitution" rights guaranteed by the United States Constitution

What militant and political Islam connection, if any, there is between Wahhabism and Salafism jihadism is disputed. Natana De Long-Bas, senior research assistant at the Prince Alwaleed Center for Muslim-Christian Understanding argues: Islamic terrorism - Osama bin Laden did not have its origins in the teachings of Ibn Abd-al-Wahhab and was not representative of Wahhabi Islam as it is practiced in contemporary Saudi Arabia, yet for the media it came to define Wahhabi Islam during the later years of bin Laden's lifetime. However unrepresentative bin Laden's global Jihad was of Islam in general and Wahhabi Islam in particular, its prominence in headline news took Wahhabi Islam across the spectrum from revival and reform to global jihad

Noah Feldman distinguishes between what he calls the deeply conservative Wahhabis and what he calls the followers of political Islam in the 1980s and 1990s, such as Egyptian Islamic Jihad Islamic Jihad and later Al-Qaeda leader Ayman al-Zawahiri. While Saudi Wahhabis were the largest funders of local Muslim Brotherhood chapters and other hard-line Islamists during this time, they opposed jihadi resistance to Muslim governments and assassination of Muslim leaders because of their belief that "the decision to wage jihad lay with the ruler, not the individual believer"

Wahhabis as well as other Islamist fundamentalists also believe in Shaia law. They extol the idea that it's the purest kind of law. Although they try to claim it's not extreme and against humanity, let's consider some of its rules, and what might happen to citizens of the United States if they were to ever rule here.

This is from an article titled, 'Islamic Law in Brief!,' written February 4, 2011, by Syed Kamran Mirza. He states, "These common laws of "Islamic Sharia" which are regularly practiced in the Islamically ruled (Sharia-based) nations with some minor variations:

1- Jihad defined as "to war against all non-Muslims to establish the religion" is the duty of every Muslim and Muslim head of state (Caliph). Muslim Caliphs who refuse jihad are in violation of Sharia and unfit to rule.

2- A Caliph can hold office through seizure of power, meaning through force.

3- The head of an Islamic State (Caliph) cannot be charged, let alone be punished for serious crimes such as murder, adultery, robbery, theft, drinking and in some cases of rape (Hudood cases) - Codified Islamic Law Vol 3 # 914C of and page 188 of Hedaya the Hanafi manual.

4- A percentage of Zakat (alms) must go towards jihad.

5- It is obligatory to obey the commands of the Caliph, even if he is unjust.

6- A Caliph must be a Muslim, a non-slave and a male.

7- The Muslim public must remove the Caliph in one case, if he rejects Islam.

8- A Muslim who leaves Islam (apostate) must be killed immediately.

9- A Muslim will be forgiven for murder of : a) an apostasy b) an adulterer c) a highway robber. Making vigilante street justice and honor killing acceptable.

10- A Muslim will not get the death penalty if he kills a non-Muslim.

11- Sharia never abolished slavery and sexual slavery and highly regulates it. A master will not be punished for killing his slave. Slavery still exists amongst Arab Muslims.

12- Sharia dictates death by stoning, beheading, for sins like killing, adultery, prostitutions; and other Quranic corporal punishments like: amputation of limbs (chopping hands and feet), floggings, beatings and other forms of cruel and unusual punishments even for the sins like: stealing, sexual promiscuity, robbery, burglary etc.

13- Non-Muslims are not equal to Muslims and must comply to Sharia (pay Zizzya: poll tax) if they are to remain safe. They are forbidden to marry Muslim women, publicly display wine or pork, recite their own religious scriptures, or openly celebrate their religious holidays or funerals. They are forbidden from building new churches or building them higher than mosques. They may not enter a mosque without permission. A non-Muslim is no longer protected if he commits adultery with a Muslim woman or if he leads a Muslim away from Islam.

14- It is a crime for a non-Muslim to sell weapons to someone who will use them against Muslims. Non-Muslims cannot curse a Muslim, say anything derogatory about Allah, the Prophet, or Islam, or expose the weak points of Muslims. However, Muslims can curse, criticize or say anything derogatory they like to the religions of others.

15- A non-Muslim cannot inherit from a Muslim.

16- Banks must be Sharia compliant and interest is not allowed.

17- No testimony in court is acceptable from people of low-level jobs, such as street sweepers or a bathhouse attendant. Women in such low level jobs such as professional funeral mourners cannot keep custody of their children in case of divorce.

18- A non-Muslim cannot rule even over a non-Muslims

minority.

19- Homosexuality is punishable by death.

20- There is no age limit for marriage of girls under Sharia. The marriage contract can take place anytime after birth and consummated at age 8 or 9.

21- Rebelliousness on the part of the wife nullifies the husband's obligation to support her, gives him permission to beat her and keep her from leaving the home.

22- Divorce is only in the hands of the husband and is as easy as saying: "I divorce you" and becomes effective even if the husband did not intend it.

23- There is no common property between husband and wife and the husband's property does not automatically go to the wife after his death.

24- A woman inherits half what a man inherits. Sister gets half of what brother gets.

25- A man has the right to have up to 4 wives and wife has no right to divorce him even if he is polygamous.

26- The dowry is given in exchange for the woman's sexual organs.

27- A man is allowed to have sex with slave women and also with women captured in battle (concubines), and if the enslaved woman is married her marriage is annulled.

28- The testimony of a woman in court is half the value of a man; that is, two women equal to one man.

29- A woman loses custody if she remarries.

30- A rapist may only be required to pay the bride-money (dowry) without marrying the rape victim.

31- A Muslim woman must cover every inch of her body which is considered "Awrah," a sexual organ. Some schools of Sharia allow the face and some don't.

32- A Muslim man is forgiven if he kills his wife caught in the act of adultery. However, the opposite is not true for women since he "could be married to the woman he was caught with."

33-It is obligatory for a Muslim to lie if the purpose is

obligatory and is known as Taqiyya (Islamic Deception). That means that for the sake of abiding with Islam's commandments, such as jihad, a Muslim is obliged to lie and should not have any feelings of guilt or shame associated with this kind of lying.

The above are clear-cut laws in Islam decided by great Imams after years of examination and interpretation of the Quran, Hadith and Mohammed's life.

34. The perpetrators of genocide, mass rape and plunder will not be punished if they repent - Codified Islamic Law Vol 1 # 13.

35. To prove rape, a woman must have 4 male witnesses. Women's testimony is not accepted - Pakistan's Hudood ordnance 7 of 1979 amended by 8B of 1980. Thousands of raped women and girls in many countries have been charged with Zena (physical relations outside marriage) and punished by Sharia courts for want of witnesses.

36. All modern music including sexually explicit music of any kind is strictly prohibited and punishable by Islamic Sharia code of justice. Only Islamic songs are allowed.

So, with all these rules in Sharia Law, what does Islam say about truth and honesty? It's required that Muslims defend Islam, even if they must be dishonest. In Mirza's article he emphasizes, "Caution! Islam permits devout Muslims to lie, cheat, and deliberately bluff non-Muslims to protect or promote his religion of Islam, anytime, anywhere. And this tactic is known as "Islamic Taqiyya" (read: Islamic deception), and was originally used by the Prophet of Islam to fool, and later subjugate and destroy enemies of Islam. As Prophet of Islam repeatedly asserted: "War is a deception" and with this holy-tactic, Prophet of Islam established his most intolerant religion of violence (by 80 plus bloody battles) which he later named as: 'religion of peace'!"

He continues, "Therefore, today's Islamists will follow

the holy path of their Prophet and will deny that—Sharia is really Islamic law! They will try to cheat by saying that, all these Sharia laws that are practiced in Saudi Arabia, Iran, Sudan, and elsewhere are not true Islamic, and they have been distorted. They also will try to fool people by saying: Saudi Arabia is ruled by King (Monarch) and Islam does not permit Kingship, etc. But, their dishonest assertion is furthest from the truth. Ancient Caliphs of Islam were nothing but the kings of ancient Islamic nations having supreme despotic and dictatorial authoritative rulers. In fact, ancient Islamic Caliphs were more despotic and brutal rulers than the present day Saudi king.

No one should be fooled into believing that these harsh and draconian laws were invented out of any wishful imagination of the so called "Islamic radicals/extremists" who came long after Muhammad. Actually, these harsh and barbarically cruelest laws came directly from the founder of Islam in his Quran and in his example in the Hadith. Almost 98% of the above samples of Sharia justice can be traced-backed to Quran and Sunnah positively. In fact, Prophet Muhammad himself actually practiced them and deliberately laid down these corporal punishments and policies to rule the ancient Islamic Caliphate. Modern kings and presidents of today's Islamic nations are doing exactly the same to emulate Islamic Prophet and those ancient rightly guided Caliphs."

In summary, the Muslim Brotherhood is a consortium to destroy everything non-Muslim on the face of the earth. It's in their doctrine. The Saudi king, who pretends to be a bystander to the Islamic revolution, is actually one of the main players to clandestinely overthrow Western ideology and civilization. That includes American citizens.

Barack Obama, who has taken an oath to protect and defend the Constitution of the United States; and whose first and primary function as commander-in-chief is to protect American citizens is failing to fulfill that responsibility. Are his actions intentional; is he part of the conspiracy? He could easily demonstrate his patriotism to the United States of America by promoting our domestic resources, by allowing more fossil fuel development in the United States and its surrounding waters. As already described earlier in this book, he and his administration have a direct plan to penalize and execute anyone who tries.

Instead, he continues to buy that same fossil fuel from Saudi Arabia, and other countries that vow to destroy us. He bows to their Saudi king then funds their plan to help them destroy us. Obviously, he was well trained in 'Islamic Taqiyya' while he was in Kenya and Indonesia.

(March 21, 2013. This is an update posted after the main draft of this book was finished. It adds to the concept of the 'evil alliance' between the United States and Saudi Arabia. I researched the information online after I heard it on a news report this morning:

"Saudi Arabia, the nation which produced 15 of the 19 hijackers in the 9/11 attacks, is about to become one of a handful of countries whose travelers can bypass normal passport controls at major U.S. airports. Sources tell the Investigative Project on Terrorism that this will mark the first time that the Saudi government will have a direct role in vetting who is eligible for getting fast-tracked for entry into the United States.

Homeland Security Secretary Janet Napolitano announced the agreement in January after meeting with Saudi Interior Minister Prince Mohammed bin Nayef. It "marks another major step forward in our partnership," Napolitano said at the time. "By enhancing collaboration with the Government of Saudi Arabia, we reaffirm our commitment to more effectively secure our two countries against evolving threats while facilitating legitimate trade and travel."

Today, while the report above was published, President

Obama's Ring: The Seat of Satan

Obama was on his visit to Israel and the Palestinian territory. Israel should beware of any peace plan proposed by Barack Obama. Israel, Christians, and the Western world must beware: the 'Ring of Satan.'

CONCLUSION

Throughout history, many powerful leaders have been considered the possible antichrist described in the Bible. During those times, their power and their ambitions seemed great indicators of that possibility, especially to the countries of their leadership and their neighbors. However, no one in the past has had the complete world stature and recognition as in our modern days.

Now, we can travel to the opposite side of the world in only a few hours, and can know exactly what's happening on that other side immediately as it's happening. Instant communication has made the world one. We are now those seven heads as one rising from the sea, the sea of mankind. That makes control of the world a more realistic possibility than any other time in history. The world being combined as one, however, is only one of the requirements of the 'beast' rising at the end times. Three other important criteria are necessary to facilitate that Armageddon. First, is power; next is deception; then turning away from God.

The world now possesses that power. When John wrote the Book of Revelation, weapons did not exist that could rain blood drops down on the battlefield. Now, a mushroom cloud lifting dried blood from a nuclear holocaust can be turned to blood rain when it reaches the heights of a misty cloud high above and merges with those droplets.

Warriors with swords and spears could not create enough death on a battlefield to cause blood to pool as deep as 'horses bridles.' Even if that many warriors were on that battlefield most would run in retreat when the battle was seen as lost. The concentration of the fallen would not be that great. Now, machine guns firing 6000 rounds a minute, missile launchers firing multiple missiles from hundreds of aircraft, and beehive rockets firing endlessly could annihilate a concentrated enemy force in only a few minutes. The survivors would have no place to run and hide; they could not retreat. What would happen to all the bodies of those who would invade Israel?

The Lord answers that question in Ezekiel 39:7.He explains, "So will I make my holy name known in the midst of my people Israel; and I will not let them pollute my holy name any more; and the heathen shall know that I am the Lord, the Holy One in Israel." Verses 11and 12 continue, "And it shall come to pass in that day, that I will give unto Gog a place there of graves in Israel, the valley of the passengers on the east of the sea: and it shall stop the noses of the passengers; and there shall they bury Gog and all his multitude: and they shall call it the Valley of Hamon-gog." "And seven months shall the house of Israel be burying of them, that they may cleanse the land."

The next requirement to create or facilitate Armageddon is deception. This concept, this idea, or this condition, when everything is considered, is what the Bible is all about. The whole lesson of the Bible is a warning not to be fooled by a deceiver, or you will lose your way to personal salvation. There are only two choices: choose salvation through Christ, or be deceived to accept the way of Satan. And, regardless what happens on the last battlefield, Heaven is still there for acceptance. But, why would a normal, sane, and reasonable person choose otherwise? Many examples and references to this 'deception' have been included in this book.

Of course there have been many deceivers throughout history. Many of those are also described in early chapters of this book. Many are listed and described to demonstrate how easy it is for rational people to be deceived - and also to show there is always a basic target of that planned deception. The deceivers always are subtle enough, as was the serpent in the Garden Eden when he deceived Eve, to prey on people's basic desires, instincts, and needs. These desires, instincts, and needs have been clearly defined and exposed. Anyone who wants to deceive has only to understand the 'Hierarchy of Needs Theory' by Abraham Maslow. Understanding this concept also helps comprehend the basic fundamentals between the two major political parties - and how unsuspecting citizens are controlled (deceived) by their leaders.

Briefly stated, Maslow describes five levels of needs that begin from the basic to the highest. The basic, physiological, is the need to survive. The next level is the need for security, followed by the need to belong. Then comes esteem or recognition, then finally at the top of the need order is self-actualization often called self-fulfillment.

Maslow suggests that a higher-order need will not be a motivating force on someone until the lower order need is essentially fulfilled. This explains how liberal politicians control more of the non-self-fulfilled citizens. They keep their thoughts focused on physical things they want and need. Then they promise they will give them an opportunity to move into the middle-class, that feeling of belonging. Never, never do the liberals encourage their followers to do something for themselves to build for themselves a feeling of self-esteem and importance; things such as getting a better education and volunteering to do something good for others in society. Perhaps our education system is the best, and most easily explained example of using a mis-directed need to expect results.

Education is America remains a dismal failure. Even with more money spent on education than ever before, and even with better educated teachers, the national drop-out rate remains near 30 percent. Furthermore, students today are less educated than students years ago having supposedly less qualified and educated teachers. Also, schools having the most spent per student ordinarily have the worst education results for those dollars spent. These are our tax dollars absolutely wasted. Not because our children are not important, but because the aims of education are not directed at the motivating needs of those students. Two factors cause this mis-direction.

First, educators are striving for self-satisfaction and self-fulfillment of their own needs, ignoring those of the children. Teachers have already gone through the first three steps of motivation: survival, safety, and belonging. They are now more influenced by their own esteem than by focusing on the cause for which is their challenge - to focus on the needs of the children. They are focused on a visible grade of which they can be proud when the children achieve them. Education's focus must be directed at the current needs of the children for those students to be responsive.

Following Maslow's ideas, that process is simple. First, children ordinarily are not concerned about survival and safety, for isn't that the purpose for parents and society? This means a student's first motivating force is the need to belong, to have that feeling of being part of his or her peers. How often does a student refer to, "my friends?"

The next level is the motivation to feel important. Even with students being driven by these two motivators, what does our elite education system focus on to encourage students to learn? They tell students they must learn these things to be successful in the future. I have something to say to these mis-directed leaders: "That future for them is not here yet. They are focused on now." They do not 'feel' that future. They 'feel' their friends and how important they are now - at this very moment.

It doesn't matter how great a teacher is at teaching advanced algebra, that teaching will be ineffective if a student is wondering what his or her friends are thinking about him or her. This should be a good clue to restructure education to make it work. That's not the purpose for this book, so I will leave it there, other than to say the more uneducated people there are in America the easier it is to deceive more people. And, I wouldn't discount the idea that it's the purpose for our failed education system. Otherwise, why would Obama appoint someone as education secretary who has already exhibited a history of dismal education leadership failure? Still, there's a third condition that must occur before those requirements in Revelation are met.

In the end times, one of the greatest forecasters of those destructive actions by the beast and his accomplices is the turning away from God by many people. Some of those things already mentioned are: haughty eyes, a lying tongue, hands that shed innocent blood, a heart that devises wicked plans, feet that make haste to run to evil, a false witness who breathes out lies, and one who sows discord among brothers. Although Obama has been very deceptive, so subtle, many of those things can still be seen in his actions and comments.

For example, his lying tongue was heard when he claimed the incident in Benghazi, where four American lives were stilled, was caused by someone's video. He knew the correct information before he made that announcement. He lied. Discovered with that lie, he called it merely a 'bump in the road.' He was deceptive again when he tried to claim that the taxes in the healthcare program were mandates. He knew they were taxes. He lied. He also lied when he said money would not be taken out of Medicare to fund his new healthcare program. He deceptively called it savings from waste. Again, he was hoping enough of his uneducated people would believe him. Being deceived, they did.

And, what about 'hands that shed innocent blood?' Has not Obama admitted authorizing missiles to be fired from drones at valid targets, then those same missiles kill other people - innocent blood - when they strike? How far removed is that from authorizing the killing of innocent blood of those who will disagree with his policies in the future? Will it matter if that innocent blood is American or foreign? That could be a heart that devises wicked plans. It could be just another 'bump in the road.'

Recently, Eric Holder issued a memo saying that the president might theoretically have the authority to order a drone strike against American citizens inside the U.S. When pressured later with a filibuster by Rand Paul, Holder issued a second statement clarifying that such a strike could only be used against a citizen who was engaged in combat. He did not elaborate on what the interpretation of 'combat' might be. Could possessing a weapon be considered 'combat' under their definition? Essentially, that question remains unanswered. The option still exists for Obama to order a drone strike to kill an American inside United States borders. If challenged, who would the stacked Supreme Court support?

Of course, Obama's greatest accomplishment of this evil described above is sowing discord among brothers. He has separated and divided our nation more than any other person or leader in the history of the United States. He has done it on the basis of economic fairness. Precisely interpreted, his words say and mean, 'those greedy rich white people are taking the food from your mouths.' That deceives his followers not to trust wealthy or middle-class people, and never to see their point of view. Is that not sowing discord among brothers?

These evils described above obviously are open to interpretation and differences of opinion depending upon whether one likes or dislikes, trusts or doesn't trust Barack Obama. There's a special abomination, however that's not open to interpretation. It's a statement of fact that he has openly expressed, himself. That statement references homosexuality. He supports and encourages it. The Bible is specifically against it and calls it an abomination.

During an interview with ABC News in May 2012, President Obama said, "I think same-sex couples should be able to get married." During his 2013 Inaugural Address he added, "Our journey is not complete until our gay brothers and sisters are treated like anyone else under the law, for if we are truly created equal, then surely the love we commit to one another must be equal as well."

Many places in the Bible condemn this act. Leviticus says, "You shall not lie with a male as with a woman; it is an abomination. Leviticus adds, "If a man lies with a male as with a woman, both of them have committed an abomination. There are similar references to women regarding homosexuality. Galations adds sexual immorality to that admonition.

With Obama's open promotion and support of homosexuality, he fills another scene prophesied to occur just before the end times - Armageddon. Perhaps that beast with seven heads rising from the sea is closer than we can imagine.

Even former president Bill Clinton has changed his support for same-sex marriage, and recently released a statement supporting it. Ah, politics is still alive, and always searching for votes anywhere they can be found.

His wife, Hillary, is expected to run for president of the United States in 2016. She is suddenly, now, supporting and promoting homosexuality, for those votes she hopes to get in the future. However, she might be in for a real surprise when she discovers Barack Obama does not plan to go quietly and compliantly at the end of his second term. Will it be a coup, or will the 22nd Amendment be overturned by his supporters? The mention of 'coup' brings forward the question of gun rights.

Our Founding Fathers recognized the possibility of a despotic and deceptive government. They realized that unaware citizens could easily be deceived to support such a leader and such a government. That's why they said we should have the right to bear arms - to own weapons. They were not proposing weapons just for hunting game and target practice. They meant serious weapons to dispel a tyranny and to keep the United States a free country. Perhaps they got the wording a little wrong with formation of the Second Amendment.

The wording should have been, "All citizens 'must' bear arms to demonstrate their love of country and their determination to keep it free." If every citizen owned a serious firearm and understood the purpose for that ownership, it's unlikely a shot would ever have to be fired to maintain our freedom. The Barack Obamas of the world, and their determined friends, the Muslim Brotherhood, wouldn't waste their time trying to conquer America. They would stay in their own Islamic countries and continue to aimlessly destroy each other - in the name of pure power control, and their Allah.

But, since we are now under this vicious threat there are two questions we must seriously consider. The first question is, 'how spellbinding is the influence of Obama's Seat of Satan ring on his coming plans and actions? The second question is, "How many will be casualties identified in this Bible reference: Revelation, Chapter 20, Verse 4:

"And I saw the souls of them that were beheaded for the witness of Jesus, and for the word of God, and which had not worshiped the beast, neither had received his mark upon their foreheads, or in their hands; and they lived and reigned with Christ a thousand years."

Americans still need two important answers.

Perhaps the answers to two questions might give a clue as to how much danger the United States is in regarding Barack Obama's actions. First, is the important question regarding Benghazi. Why did the Obama administration allow four Americans to be slaughtered by Islamic radicals without showing any interest in offering aid or support? There are only three possible answers to this question:

First; Obama was afraid he would upset his Islamic cohorts. His friends might think he was no longer supporting them, in which case the Muslim Brotherhood had to be involved.

Second; a mission was underway that would expose an operation that Obama wanted to keep secret. If it were a secret mission, then normal procedure is to have a backup operations plan to prevent a catastrophe. Why didn't they execute the backup plan? The military would not act in a dangerous situation such as this event without a backup escape plan. I was in the military for 20 years; don't let anyone tell you otherwise. I was personally involved with a serious backup plan. I know the military drill.

Third; Obama was a political coward. The Benghazi event occurred during his 2012 campaign for president of the United States. Sacrificing those four American citizens was better for him than to take any kind of action that would result in more American casualties. A major event would have been a political setback. He might have thought it would be politically safer to just 'let those four be sacrificed' for the sake of his political future. A true military decision would have been to do whatever it takes to save American lives. He failed to do that. The next day - the very next day - he went

241

on a fund-raising trip to Las Vegas.

Why didn't Hillary Clinton tell the whole truth about the Benghazi event? Because, that might be a negative mark against her if she plans to campaign for president in 2016. Apparently she thought it was safer just to shout, "What difference does it make how they died?"

The loss of high-powered weapons in 'Operation Fast and Furious' is another serious event that must have more answers; more honest answers. The Obama administration, including Barack Obama, personally, seems to have no interest in answering the cause of an innocent man's death. Obama will not let anyone in his administration even speak or whisper anything negative about any of his Muslim friends, yet he functions as if he cares nothing about an American citizen's life.

Where are those AK-47s? Why were they lost - unaccounted for, even though that was supposedly the purpose for the operation? Are they really lost, or are they hidden, waiting to be used against more innocent Americans when the right conditions arise for the Muslim Brotherhood to take some final action to 'destroy America' as they plan? I realize this question sounds absurd, but it's a question that should not be discounted until the administration gives a better answer.

Now, in closing, here comes the most important question. Do our elected members in Congress have enough interest and enough courage to really and seriously investigate these matters and attempt to preserve the America our Founding Fathers gave us? God help us if they don't. The Islamists say, proclaim, shout, that they will destroy us and our way of life. Should we not believe them?

And, who is Barack Hussein Obama? Is he one of us; or is he one of them? Understanding the background of the serpents on his ring gives an excellent clue.

Finally:

How could Jim Jones deceive so many people
and 909 died?

How could David Koresh deceive so many people
and 83 died?

How could Marshall Applewhite deceive so many people
and 39 people died?

How could Barack Obama deceive so many people
and - ?

How can American citizens feel safe and be secure
led by a man who hates and disrespects
America and its Constitution?

God Bless America.

Obama's Ring: The Seat of Satan

Greatest Quotes

of

Our Time

———————————

Michelle Obama

February 18, 2008

"For the first time in my adult life I am proud of my country."

(Age 44)

Barack Obama

March 9, 2008

"We are no longer a Christian nation - at least not just."

Nancy Pelosi

March 9, 2010

"We have to pass the bill so that you can find out what is in it."

Hillary Clinton

January 23, 2013

"What difference, at this point, does it make?"

Obama's Ring: The Seat of Satan

About the Author

Will Clark's author experiences began by writing inspection and evaluation reports in the U.S. Air Force. He is a retired Air Force officer and a Vietnam veteran, serving in Saigon from 1966 to 1967. His other overseas assignments include Misawa, Japan and Ankara, Turkey.

In 1995, he authored a book, How to Learn, as a county-wide study skills project to encourage students to improve their grades in DeSoto County, Mississippi. Education supporters printed and distributed four thousand copies. He also wrote a weekly education column for a local newspaper, The Desoto County Tribune.

His next published book was School Bells and Broken Tales, a parody of nursery rhyme characters, also a motivation and education book for children. His other books include Shades of Retribution, a historical novel, and Simply Success, a motivation guide for students and employees.

His action novels include a trilogy based on Atlantis and crystals. The first book is titled: The Atlantis Crystal. The second book is titled: She Waits In Atlantis. The third is: Return to Atlantis. This trilogy is based on his travels while assigned to Turkey, site of the ancient city of Troy. While in Turkey, he visited the ruins of Troy and the seven biblical churches described in the Bible Book of Revelation.

His last book, 666: Mark of the Beast, is a sequel to his previous book, America 20XX: The New World Order.

Clark and his wife, Marie, live in Diamondhead, Mississippi, where they play golf with many friends.

Obama's Ring: The Seat of Satan

Other Books by the Author

Synopsis
AMERICA 20XX:
THE NEW WORLD ORDER

Vision is the new federal constabulary force established by U.S. President Arabar when funding is not available for states and municipalities to fund their own police and security forces. This major funding crisis results from the continuing rise in oil prices. Oil prices are controlled by an Islamic king, King Rayeed, determined to execute a successful jihad in America. He knows he must destroy America's strength before he can attack his final target, Israel.

President Arabar, conspiring with King Rayeed, refuses to use American resources to avert the crisis. Pretending to increase development of ethanol to counter that crisis, Arabar creates a food shortage crisis.

Vision increases its numbers by using jihadists smuggled into the United States through the porous Texas and Arizona borders. Their first act is to confiscate registered weapons from gun owners. Then they plan to rush in more Vision troops by ship to expand control. They are free to act as security forces because President Arabar has ordered our military forces to stand down and be prepared to guard against a foreign aerial attack.

The Texas governor, cooperating with Arizona Governor

Ann Melody, enlists the help of his good friend, a retired Marine named Carl Brannan, to slow the invasion. Brannan forms a network of old friends throughout America to defeat the invasion. Their first goal is to thwart Vision's efforts to confiscate personal weapons. They do this by giving receipts for the weapons using Vision's receipt documents. Brannan and his three partners continue to harass Vision departments and installations, giving hope to others that someone is resisting the jihad.

Eventually, Brannan and his group are captured. To quell all resistance, President Arabar plans their public hanging in the National Mall. He is pleased when a million citizens show up to witness the event. Just before the levers are pulled, a million citizens point their weapons at Arabar and the hundred jihadists guarding the event.

Given the option of facing charges of treason or exiling himself to another country, Arabar chooses exile to King Rayeed's country. When he arrives, he gets the same homecoming as Saddam Hussein's sons-in-law. Before he left the United States he signed documents contrary to Islamic principles and beliefs.

Governor Ann Melody is elected president to reestablish a government based on the U.S. Constitution. John Marker, the Texas Governor, returns to Texas, to his favorite fishing hole.

Synopsis
666: MARK OF THE BEAST

This story depicts a scenario of how and why the Battle of Armageddon might evolve in the near future. Although fictional, it incorporates current events and international relationships to show this evil and evolving situation. It begins with the question: Who is most likely to initiate that apocalyptic battle against Israel? That answer is simple, by considering who wants to destroy Israel at this very moment. It's the radical Islamic nations. They will stop at nothing to destroy Israel.

The leader of that battle will be the one-world leader at that time. This means the one-world leader must be a Muslim or a Muslim supporter. Muslims might even consider him their Messiah, while he pretends to be the other Messiah. That leader is described in the Bible as the 'Deceiver.'

When his reign begins he will be lauded as a 'man of peace' and will be respected and revered by all nations. His power will begin by becoming leader of the ten European nations (the countries of the north) that once were part of the Roman Empire.

Through treaties, sanctions, and threats, he will disarm countries and make them vulnerable to his real plans of destruction. He will also initiate his 'mark' to allow people to transact business. Without his mark, people will not be allowed to buy or sell items. The mark will be an interactive computer chip that will identify each person as a follower of the one-world leader. Once he has computer control over every person, he will evolve into the 'Beast' and begin his inhuman acts against humanity.

This book considers three situations. First, citizens must decide if they want to accept the Beast's mark so they can continue to live normally. They ask how can they live like humans if they can't buy or sell anything. Second, if they refuse the mark how can they survive, especially when the Beast's enforcers are trying to track them down and kill them. The Beast is enforcing his condition of 'homogeneity' whereby the population must be controlled within acceptable environmental factors. Third, the Beast must destroy America's strength to allow his final attack on Israel. What will happen to Israel? What will happen to America? The deadly Battle of Armageddon is the final scene in the book.

End